Autumn Passage

Autumn Passage

Renae Angeroth

ISBN 978-0-578-03337-2

Front cover art: *Autumn Passage*, acrylic painting (digitally-enhanced) by Jane Robinette © 2009 Jane Robinette

Back cover photograph © Renae Angeroth

To my parents,

Who gave me their story

To give to my children

Prologue

September 27

Dad's first round of chemotherapy was powerful and unexpectedly harsh for a man who rarely even had a cold. He wasn't prepared for the high fever, nausea, and aching joints. When he could no longer keep food or drink in his system, his doctors admitted him into the hospital for intravenous hydration and close monitoring.

"Do you want us to use any machines or life-saving measures, Charles?" The nurse asked Dad upon admittance. "You know, in case things go bad."

Dad didn't hesitate with his answer.

"No."

If this was the treatment, he thought, he'd rather be dead. "Don't do anything to bring me back."

The nurse immediately looped a brightly colored band around his wrist to alert any medical staff that this patient was DNR, Do Not Resuscitate.

Once saline was pumped into his system, along with two pints of whole blood, Dad's strength returned, his fever cooled, and he was able to tolerate foods like Jell-O and beef broth from the hospital cafeteria.

By the end of the third day, Dad was much more lucid and felt better prepared to face his cure. Bored, he looked around the room for something to occupy his time, and his gaze landed on the bracelet attached to his wrist. He studied it, wondering how the nurses would remove it. His curiosity turned to panic when he realized what it meant. Now he wanted it off.

Frantically, he began to rip, tug, even claw at the plastic strip, trying to pry it from his body lest one of his doctors arrive too soon and pull a white sheet over Dad's head. The plastic was strong. Dad used his teeth, but the band still held. Finally, he scrounged through the dresser drawers next to his bed until he found a pair of fingernail clippers from his pants pocket. In two snips, he freed himself of the death sentence wrapped around his hand.

It wasn't that Dad was afraid of dying. He just wasn't finished living yet.

Driving to the farm takes a little more than two hours from my house in Des Moines. As I head west, the sun melts behind the dust storms stirred by the autumn harvest. My trip today is just a short one before the real adventure begins.

Tomorrow I travel with my parents to the western United States where we will spend eight days together sightseeing and visiting some of their old friends. While I'm away, a stack of papers at work will grow exponentially on my desk. My Itzhak Perlman ticket will go unused, even though the rest of my family will enjoy the violin concert. Rob will successfully transport our three children, Elisabeth, Clarissa, and Eric, to their soccer games, music practices, and early-morning or after-school activities. In addition to other missed events and responsibilities, I'll miss out on the day my son becomes a teenager. Still, it's important that I be with my parents this coming week.

My little Honda Civic turns into the driveway of my childhood home, passing the hill where we used to travel to outer space inside of an old corn picker. I park on the south side of the power pole, or what used to be first base in our makeshift baseball field. The cottonwood tree was second base, the water pump was third, and any empty feed sack was a good substitute for home plate because we could move it around a little to give us a head start toward the bases.

For most of their married lives, Mom and Dad farmed these 360 acres of rich rolling hills in western Iowa. Less than ten years ago, Dad made the transition from active farmer to retired gentleman. Now he plays relaxed rounds of golf with old friends and dabbles in his wood workshop. An oversized garden in the summers keeps him busy, as do the constant conversations when he delivers his fresh produce to all the neighbors.

Dad never stood more than five foot seven, and his frame continues to shrink with age. A round face and protruding belly divulge his love for heavy, rich food. Still, despite his short, stubby legs, he keeps a brisk stride.

For her fun, my mother has no fewer than six sewing machines connected to three computers. She loves creating new projects and generously shares her sewing passion with friends and granddaughters. She has tried to teach me, but I don't have either the patience or the inclination. Mostly, I don't have her talent.

With no concern for appearances around the farm, Mom's wardrobe consists of threadbare shirts and double-knit pants with elastic unraveling at the waist. But I don't underestimate her when she slips into a dress, steps into a pair of heels, and applies her lipstick. She strikes a very attractive pose, even for a seventy-one-year-old woman.

"Hello, sweetie." Mom hugs me just before I pull my two small suitcases from the car. Usually, both parents meet me, but tonight it's only Mom. She holds the door as I step inside.

I set my purse and bags down in the entry area where a bookshelf full of framed family portraits of the grandchildren stands to my left and the back of a Copenhagen-blue floral sofa is on my right. Directly opposite the couch in the main part of the living room are two overstuffed recliners decorated with different, not necessarily coordinating, fabrics. A small television perches on top of a light oak cabinet recently crafted by Dad. The primary source of heat, a black wood stove propped up on a metal box, partitions the living room from the kitchen.

As I take off my jacket and drape it over the back of the sofa, I see my father in his chair with both eyes closed. He's quiet but not asleep. Chemotherapy has left him bald, and his arms, normally well tanned from long days in the fields, have turned shadowy white. His once-strong body now melts into his recliner.

"Hey, Dad. How you doing?" Obviously, Dad was not "doing" very much of anything today.

"Pretty good, Rin," he answers without opening his eyes. Only my family calls me "Rin." Not Ren, the first three letters of my name, and not "wren," a reference to the tiny, delicate songbird. No, I am "Rin," the same as the dog in the old television series, "Rin-Tin-Tin."

Mom's vacuum sweeper stands at attention in the middle of the living room. She abandoned it when she saw me coming down the lane. She also has dusted the furniture, wiped down the kitchen floor, stacked mail and magazines under a side table, and cleared off all the counters. She performs this cleaning ritual before leaving on any vacation. No matter where they go, the house first must be tidy. I confess I do the same thing.

Mom returns to her vacuum to roll up the power cord, but before she can finish, she is interrupted again.

"Zola, bring me my medicine, will ya?"

Mom pushes the vacuum back to the hall closet and heads to the kitchen for Dad's pills.

"Have you taken your antibiotic yet, Charles?" Mom calls out casually to clarify which medicine Dad is requesting. Alarm bells ring inside my head when I hear the word *antibiotic*.

"What are the antibiotics for, Dad?" I ask cautiously. "Do you have an infection?"

Either too tired to answer or deliberately avoiding the subject, he doesn't respond.

Mom speaks for him. "Well, a little one, but he's had it all week, and he just has one more day on the pills."

No one mentioned his new medical condition to me despite the number of times we spoke on the phone this week.

"Ten days of antibiotic, and it hasn't knocked it out yet? Are you sure we should even be going?" Given that we will soon be en route to relatively isolated locations, places where hospitals and urgent medical care facilities don't exist, I believe my concerns are legitimate.

"He really just has a slight fever now," Mom says.

"How high?" I need specifics.

"Only about a hundred or so. It's much better than it was." Her words fail to assuage me.

Even though he keeps his eyes closed behind his oversized aviator glasses, Dad senses my brown eyes, the same color as his, staring him down.

"We're going," he says firmly, establishing no need for further discussion.

Malignant fibrous histiocytoma is the ugly, polysyllabic name for Dad's cancer. The disease initially began as a bump on his right shin nearly three years ago. Surgery removed the soft tissue tumor in his leg, and chemotherapies, despite their intense and vociferous side effects, kept the cancer from growing.

Gradually, the prescription poison grew less effective and the cancer returned. Dark spots on the x-ray film are not only visible in his leg, but now grow in his lungs. Once strong and fiercely determined in his attitude and daily living, my father now submits in exhaustion.

Dad recognizes the physical deterioration betraying his body. If there are any foods he wants to taste, places he wants to visit, or adventures he seeks to experience, he must act now.

What Dad wants is to attend a navy reunion next week in Idaho, detouring through Yellowstone and Grand Teton National Parks, places he has always longed to see. A special bonus for him would be to see a bear, a big fierce grizzly that in one look evokes both majesty and terror that could scare the cancer clean out of a human body.

My parents first told me about their plans six months ago, during one of our weekly phone conversations. At that time, they hoped to drive their car the entire route, through Nebraska and Colorado, with stops in Montana and Wyoming to visit friends.

"I want to take every back road, stop at every small town, every rodeo, every farm store and implement dealer along the way," Dad said. "Even try some wild game if I get the chance."

Their proposed itinerary would challenge even a healthy person. Although the cancer was invading his lungs, the throbbing pain behind his right knee was increasing and would be the real obstacle to their travel plans. He controls the pain with very expensive tablets and a morphine patch on his back. The medication works primarily by making him drowsy, less focused or alert.

"You don't think driving will be a problem?" I asked, remembering the pharmaceutical instruction warning against operating heavy equipment while taking the medication.

"Nah, I drive all the time. I just use my right foot for the gas and brake with my left," he brushed off casually. "It works just fine."

His use of the word "fine" seemed highly subjective.

"What about all that pain medication? You'll want to be awake when you drive on those mountain roads."

"Well, that's something I'll just work around," he said, as if we were merely discussing road construction.

I wondered if someone should go with them, someone like me, maybe. I could prevent Dad from driving as well as relieve them of planning all the minor details. Rob and I visited Yellowstone five or six years ago with our own three children, and I remembered having to make reservations with a special park concessionaire and ordering lots of road maps.

The parks were beautiful, but we didn't have enough time or patience with the kids for serious exploration. I would enjoy seeing it again. I also wouldn't mind a brief escape from the demands and monotony of my daily routine.

The greatest motivation for wanting to tag along, though, was to spend precious time with my parents. Not just Dad, but Mom and Dad, together. We could have deep discussions as we explore and appreciate the rugged western landscapes. This would be our last opportunity to share our personal beliefs, ideas, and philosophies with each other.

"Maybe I should go with you." The idea left my mind and moved to my lips before I could stop it. "I could chauffeur you around so you won't have to do all the driving and can enjoy the scenery."

"Yeah, okay if you want to." Dad surprised me by agreeing so readily. Relinquishing control of this kind would not be easy for one who preferred the driver to the passenger seat. Maybe he didn't believe my proposal to accompany them was serious.

But I was serious, and I spent the next two months working out the arrangements. No matter how hard I crunched the miles, however, I realized I couldn't be away for as long as they had planned.

Dad wanted to drive the open road, so I was hesitant to suggest air travel. Also, the cramped tight spaces of an airplane increased the risk of a fellow traveler unknowingly injuring Dad's leg. Finally, the logistics of shepherding him through airport security procedures were daunting. If we had any hope of returning to Iowa by Thanksgiving, part of our journey had to be by plane.

On Dad's seventy-third birthday, his second birthday since the diagnosis of his terminal cancer, I drove to the farm to celebrate the milestone with my parents. As they were already in a good mood, I used the opportunity to entice them into alternative transportation options.

"Dad, is flying completely out of the question?" I approached gingerly. "I'd make sure you had a bulkhead seat at the front of the airplane and also make sure that nobody accidentally bumps your leg." I showed him on paper just how many hours those miles would take to drive.

"No, no it's not out of the question," he said with deliberateness. "If we could get a good deal, I'd do it."

He actually seemed open to the idea. Maybe he was already tired and realized the limitations of his endurance. Before I could rationalize his answer any further, he clarified his response.

"In fact," he said, "given the current price of gasoline, we're probably better off if we do fly."

After forty-three years of being his daughter, I should have realized that Dad's ultimate decision would not be about physical limitations or sentimentality, but about money. Dad insists on making this trip, but he won't spend one penny more than necessary to travel from Iowa to Idaho.

"And one room should be plenty fine for the three of us, don't you think?" Mom asked me. My eyelashes reached up to my brows. Mom and Dad conceded the air travel. I couldn't argue for separate rooms.

During this same visit in late August, Dad was still fairly mobile. He used his walker outside, but he was able to limp around the house without extra assistance. In the five weeks since we made those plans, his condition has changed dramatically. A wheelchair is required for any extended distance, indoors or out, and he is never without his walker. I didn't take these limitations into consideration when I made our lodging reservations.

Genuinely concerned that Dad doesn't have the strength for this journey, I call my older sister, Rhonda, for guidance.

"Did you know that Dad has a fever?" This is more of a statement than a question. "It's over a hundred."

"Yes, I've heard," Rhonda calmly answers. "I've talked to them both. He really wants to do this trip. I don't think you can talk him out of it. And if that's what he wants to do, I think you should go ahead. It'll be all right."

Easy for her to say. She won't be the one who has to arrange emergency helicopter transportation from Old Faithful.

This past Labor Day, Rhonda and her husband, Mike, organized a crew of family and friends to pour a concrete parking pad and sidewalk for my parents. Now Dad can walk on an even surface from the car to the house thanks to them. I didn't help with the concrete, and the least I can do is escort my parents out west.

Rhonda will be our taxi to and from the Omaha airport tomorrow, a twenty-minute car ride across the Missouri River. Given that the flight leaves at 7:55 a.m., Rhonda and I agree we'll have ample time if she arrives by half past six.

Mom overhears my part of the conversation and looks skeptical.

"We have to get him," tipping her head toward my sleeping father in the other room, "a wheelchair and all that rigmarole. That's making it a little tight, don't you think?"

"Can you pick us up at 6:15 instead?" My sister understands the change in plans without me having to explain.

"I'll see you tomorrow then," she says before hanging up.

Dad continues dozing in his chair, the upholstery worn thin from his hair and arms rubbing against it. He props up his legs in front of him for better circulation and doesn't even flinch when the telephone rings minutes later.

My younger sister, Cynthia, is phoning to wish us a fun and safe trip. "Well, thanks," I say, "but I don't know how fun it's going to be with him so sick." I try to keep my voice down so Mom, who is rinsing dishes in the sink, doesn't hear me.

"Did you know Dad is fighting some sort of infection?" I ask Cyn, walking away from the kitchen.

I put her through the same series of questions I covered with Rhonda, hoping that if I ask enough people, at least one person will agree with me that the trip should be cancelled.

"Yeah, I know," she answers compliantly. "He's had it for a few days now. I thought he was better."

"Mom thinks he is, but he's sleeping right now, and his face is pretty flushed."

Like my other sister, Cyn supports the decision to travel tomorrow. "This is what he wants to do. This is something he needs to do."

I finish the futile telephone conversation and review the itinerary with Mom at the kitchen table. With eyes closed, Dad listens in from the other side of the wood stove.

"We go from Omaha to Phoenix, change planes, fly to Salt Lake City, rent a car, and then drive north to Idaho Falls where we will spend the first night."

After providing enough details to satisfy them both, Mom folds up the western states maps and places them in her carry-on bag. She then double checks that she has unplugged her computers in the sewing room.

I stand between the kitchen and living room with my back to the wood stove, absorbing the heat it offers. In front of me is an unfamiliar old man, hands folded across his chest and cheeks glowing from the fever. With such compromised strength, he'll only see a fraction of the parks and won't have much time to spend with his friends. What if he breaks his hip or needs another blood transfusion? The trip will steal all his remaining strength to fight the cancer. Given the risks involved and the limited amount we will actually see and do, I seriously question the value of this trip.

The evening nap gives Dad the energy he needs to prepare for bed. He manages most of it on his own but requires Mom's help to pull off his boots and socks. She kneels to loosen his laces crossed around the metal hooks. With the gentleness one shows to a newborn infant, she rocks the worn chocolate-colored leather boot side to side until it slides from his right foot. More quickly but with equal delicateness, she removes his left boot and sock. After swallowing his evening medicine, Dad hobbles off to the bedroom, grunting to let us know he has made it safely to the bed.

"Don't forget to clean my walker, will ya?" he yells from the bedroom. He suggested to Mom earlier how nice it would be if it were cleaned for the trip, knowing full well that Mom, not Dad, would do the cleaning.

At 10:30 p.m., my mother and I wash down the four-legged contraption using bleach and a chemical spray whose contents label fell off years ago. Purchased at a garage sale, the silver walker has no wheels or neon yellow tennis balls attached to the bottom like some models. Scratches and dents make it impossible to look new, but it smells clean.

Despite the fact that it will never leave his hands, Dad insists that his name be visible on the walker. Mom dutifully places an adhesive return address label underneath the right handle, a label mailed to Dad courtesy of a disabled veterans group. She also writes his name in permanent marker under the stainless-steel tubing that connects the pieces, just in case the adhesive label should fall away.

When there remains nothing for me to clean or personalize, I take my smaller suitcase into the spare bedroom adjacent to that of my parents. I settle in between a set of pale peach sheets, linens I recognize from my high school days. When I turn off the lights,

I become keenly aware of the scent from the wood fire and the sounds of my mother's last-minute chores seeping through the bedroom door.

My parents are practical in every other aspect of their life, yet they deny their instincts by insisting on this trip. Anxiety and nerves call me to be the voice of reason and cancel our plans before catastrophe arises. But I agree with my sisters. We can see that Dad is losing to the cancer and won't have another opportunity to take this or any other excursion. He must go now while he still has some residual stamina, before the pain medications lose all usefulness, and before this disease ultimately defeats him.

Based on what I've seen tonight, I'll need as much rest as possible before tomorrow's adventures begin.

Wednesday

September 28

It's 4:45 a.m. The din created by Dad scraping ashes from the wood stove suggests that I should be awake and already out of bed. Both he and Mom are finishing final tasks before we leave. A leaky pipe requires that Dad turn off the water to the bathroom. He also checks and rechecks the locks on the doors. Mom unplugs the toaster and dries the breakfast dishes. A double and triple check of all prescription as well as over-the-counter medicine assures us that every capsule and tablet is accounted for in Mom's carry-on bag.

Dad has on his going-to-town clothes, a light blue jacket over his blue and green plaid shirt, and a white T-shirt next to his skin. A hat always sits on his head when he leaves the house. Typically, he uses a seed corn or farm implement cap, but because this is a special day, he wears one without any advertisement at all. Tucked away in his suitcase is an official navy reunion hat he will punch into shape and place on his shiny head when we reach Idaho.

Dad's jeans are dark blue new, not faded or worn, as is the current fashion trend for my children. Instead of his work boots, he wears caramel brown Rockports on his feet. Customarily, a pair of pliers hangs from a worn leather pouch attached to his belt, convenient and ready to adjust farm machinery, hammer down stray nails, or remove loose teeth. As he believes he won't have any need for his favorite tool while he is away, he leaves the pliers in the table drawer next to his chair.

Mom has changed her appearance, too. Her light blue slacks match her jacket with flowers embroidered on the front. Her hair was recently permed to make her appear "presentable" as she says. A light application of make-up polishes the look.

We finish shutting down the house, and the rooms are as clean as they ever will be. Our luggage waits at attention by the front door, but more than a half an hour remains before Rhonda's expected arrival.

"I think we should have a word of prayer before we leave," Dad says.

A prayer was always said in our home before any significant event, or sometimes just to go to church. The tradition was for us to join hands while Dad prayed for safety and strength for whatever was ahead.

My parents have strong religious beliefs. They practice their religion daily by acting as lay ministers, youth leaders, volunteering at the local social service center, and serving on conservation boards. Before his own diagnosis, Dad enjoyed helping out at a camp for children with cancer.

As a child and even into young adulthood, I was arrogantly confident about my faith in God, Jesus, and my purpose in the world. With age and life experience, hesitation seeped into my credo until eventually all the basic concepts I ever believed were soggy with uncertainty. Some ideas continue to be attractive and appeal to a strong desire to believe the religion of my parents. But beliefs are difficult to maintain with ever-present doubt.

I've never discussed my lapsing religious philosophy with either of my parents. Rejecting that which is literally sacred to them would serve no purpose. Instead, on this morning, I grasp hands with my father on my right and my mother to my left. As we stand in the middle of the living room underneath the ceiling fan, Dad thanks his Heavenly Father for the opportunity to take this trip, asks for strength in the miles ahead, and trusts implicitly that his god will ensure our safe return.

Regardless of my current faith, or lack thereof, I am humbled by both the sincerity and words of his prayer.

Rhonda anticipated we would be ready before our agreed-upon time. Just after six a.m., her Cadillac rolls down the lane, a relatively nice car compared to what our parents used to park in front of this house.

As a farmer, Dad required a decent truck, but cars weren't as critical. We thought nothing of our family of six packing into the cab of the pickup when Dad drove animals to the Omaha stockyards. If we stayed home, we missed a chance for an ice cream cone on the return trip.

I can't count the number of times we were late for a school practice or event because of a bad transmission, flat tire, or blown gasket in our car. We once owned a maroon AMC Rambler, fully functional in every way except for reverse gear. The trick was to be careful where we parked. After one particularly embarrassing episode on the side of the road, I vowed that when I became an adult, I would earn enough money to afford reliable transportation.

The quality of vehicle improved dramatically after all of us kids graduated from high school. Dad kept an eye on those neighbors who had a reputation for prudent driving skills and regular maintenance of their automobiles. When the neighbor drove a new make or model drove past the farm, Dad beat the competition to the dealer to bargain for what he knew would be the best deal on the used-car market.

In the predawn light, we make our way to Rhonda's car. Under Mom's keen supervision, Dad shuffles along using his walker. Rhonda and I carry the luggage. Usually Dad does the driving, and now with his sore leg, he uses the steering wheel to leverage himself into the car. Today he must learn how to enter a vehicle in a whole new way.

First, he tries to sit in the backseat behind the driver, but the space is too small for him to keep his right leg straight. After heavy sighs and contorted facial grimaces, Dad tries the front passenger seat instead. Though there's more room, a trash container permanently attached to the side panel obstructs him from fully extending his leg.

Mom reaches in to assist, but Dad shoos her off with an unpleasant tone.

"If I could just drive, I could get in here a lot easier," he says.

To her credit my sister pretends not to hear. We watch as Dad alternates his grip on the dashboard to the roof of the car and struggles to maneuver himself into Rhonda's vehicle. Pushing as far back into the seat as possible, he cautiously manipulates his right leg on top of his left foot and uses the strength of his good leg to lift both limbs. Finally, he gingerly moves past the trash container and is completely in the car.

"There," he exhales loudly. Mom checks to make sure both feet are safely in before she pushes the car door shut.

I stow Dad's fresh-smelling walker in the trunk with the rest of our luggage and check my watch. Six thirty. I check again, not believing that we just spent a half an hour fitting Dad into the car. In addition to the hotel accommodations, I now consider that we might need different transportation options as well.

Rhonda pulls up to the curb at the airport, and I spring out of the backseat to retrieve our belongings from the trunk. I thought I had packed light with only a small suitcase to check through and a smaller piece to carry with me. Mom and Dad have packed all of their things together in one tiny suitcase. My only concession is that Mom's purse is larger than mine.

Mom opens Dad's door and helps to guide him out of his seat.

"Move your foot over a little this way, Charles," she encourages him.

With the same delicateness Dad used to enter the car, he now scoots and turns and twists until he stands upright with his hands on top of the door. I hand Mom the walker, and she places it into position for Dad. With her help, he hobbles onto the curb.

A tall, thin skycap with graying hair brings a wheelchair for Dad, a stainless steel model trimmed in black. The leather seat and back fold in the middle until we pull the chair taut. Two large back wheels carry most of the weight while the smaller disks in front wobble until they find their sense of direction. Steel footplates adjust to suit the passenger.

Dad eases himself into the chair with Mom at his side. I pick up the bags to follow.

"You guys have a great trip." Rhonda gives us farewell hugs, but she leaves me with a feeling of abandonment as she drives back into the lines of traffic.

"Where you folks headed?" asks the skycap whose badge identifies him as Carl.

"Salt Lake City," says Dad.

"Yes, but we are going to Phoenix first," Mom clarifies.

Carl leads us into the terminal to the ticket counter.

"Okay. You give me your driver's licenses, and I'll get your tickets." Carl's request sounds almost like a ransom demand, but we don't hesitate to comply.

More quickly and easily than we could have managed, Carl proceeds to the head of the line, checks our bags, and secures all of our boarding passes for the entire trip. When he has the passes in hand, Carl pilots us upstairs to the security checkpoint. Mom and I walk through the electronic porthole while Carl extricates Dad from the wheelchair. Mom holds on to the walker as we watch Dad proceed through the checkpoint.

"I need you to step over here, sir." The security officer instructs Dad to stand with his feet inside the yellow outline of two shoes on the floor. The officer intends to be gentle, but Dad balks when the pat down reaches his right knee.

"Sorry, sir. I'll try to be more careful." The officer pulls back slightly and briefly, then proceeds to search Dad's midsection. The security wand begins to chirp.

Three summers ago, Dad strung an electric fence around the perimeter of his field of prized sweet corn. The idea was to protect it from marauding raccoons. On the top rung of a rickety ladder against a rotting wooden post, Dad reached for the last insulator. Predictably, the ladder tipped, and Dad crashed to the ground onto his right hip.

He managed to pull himself onto his four-wheeler and aim for the house. Rather than wait for an ambulance, however, he insisted that Mom drive him to the hospital. The punishment for his impatience came at the emergency room when he realized he was virtually paralyzed. With gentle cajoling, the emergency room crew inched him from the front seat onto a waiting gurney.

After surgery to rebuild his hip with stainless steel parts, we inspected all of Dad's other injuries, the secondary scratches and bruises that covered his arms and forehead. He also showed us where he hit his right shin, the exact location where his cancer would begin to grow a few years later.

"This is from his doctor." Mom hands the security guard a letter that describes the metal pins that now live on Dad's right side.

"Okay, you're clear." The guard pronounces Dad as a safe passenger.

Carl finishes pushing Dad a short distance to our gate and pulls up the brake handle.

"Oh, thank you so much. You are a saint," Mom gushes and presses three one-dollar bills into Carl's hand before he walks away.

"I got to go to the bathroom before I get on that plane," Dad says.

I'm confronted with a third factor I didn't consider when making plans for this trip. A common side effect of chemotherapy is chronic constipation. The condition is further exacerbated by his pain medication and inability to exercise.

With his walker lying across the wheelchair armrests, I push him to the bathroom directly across from our gate. Holding onto his walker makes him feel more useful but causes me to underestimate the width of his chair.

"Oh, excuse me," I say as I bang the elbows and legs of passengers in the terminal. "Sorry."

At the bathroom, I unfold Dad's walker and set it in front of him. The brakes of the wheelchair are locked into place as I pull the left footrest up and out of his way. With his weight balanced on his left leg and armrests, Dad cautiously raises himself out of the chair. Once steady, I draw the chair away, slowly, literally pulling the right footrest out from under him. In this manner, he never has to actually move his right foot. The entire procedure takes about three minutes, and he still hasn't reached the bathroom.

While I wait for Dad, I scan the terminal for a mailbox. I need to send Eric's birthday card today in order for him to receive it by Friday.

"Is there an outgoing mail box around here?" I ask the man at the bookstand. He stands and looks around just as I have done already.

"No," he says. "I don't see one."

I'll try again in Utah.

Dad returns from the bathroom and sinks back into the safety of the wheelchair's black leather seat. Although we have more than an hour before our plane departs, we camp at the seats adjacent to the gate door, ready for a swift departure.

A sign at the gate instructs travelers with special needs to secure a blue preboarding pass. When the agent appears, I ask for and receive the special pass without giving any explanation. The rest of the wait is used to study other passengers milling about the terminal, men and women who have no idea how easy life is with two good legs. At least, I never thought about such things until today.

"Good morning, ladies and gentlemen." The sound of the agent's announcement sends an unexpected surge of adrenaline to my heart.

"We are just about to start boarding Southwest Flight 597 to Phoenix. We'd like to preboard all first-class passengers and those who need special assistance."

No one mistakes us for first-class passengers, but no one challenges Dad's need for special assistance. I roll Dad to the door and hand over the blue plastic tag with our boarding passes to a man dressed in a navy blue shirt and khaki pants. The Southwest employee, whose nametag is obstructed, drives Dad down the jet bridge, oblivious to the pain inflicted each time he crosses one of the horizontal joints. He has no concept or care for why this old man sits in a wheelchair in the first place. Despite the brutal jarring, Dad stays quiet. If either Mom or I had been pushing him, we would have heard about it.

Southwest Airlines does not provide seat assignments. Because we are first to board, we greedily claim the first three seats at the front of the plane. Not only are they the closest, they also have extra legroom, perfect for Dad.

"I don't want to get clear in there," Dad says pointing to the window seat, "but I don't want anyone to slam into me either."

He plants himself in the middle, watching protectively as the agent tags his walker and stows it deep inside the underbelly of the aircraft.

After our seat belts are securely fastened and we are confident about how to adjust our oxygen masks, the flight attendant asks us to identify the exit closest to us.

"Where's our exit, Rin?" Dad asks.

The front door is nearest, of course, but if for some reason that is blocked, we would have to exit thirteen rows behind us. I look at the exit. I look at Dad.

"We wouldn't make it." We both laugh, but we both know it is true.

Although we certainly have our differences, I'm a lot like my father. I was the one child born with straight black hair and equally dark eyes while my brother and two sisters favored Mom's Danish heritage and much lighter complexion. In addition to Dad's coloring, I also received his DNA for a short, stubby frame and round face.

We also seem to share a similar sense of humor. Recently, I caught myself using an old joke I had once heard Dad tell. Only after I finished did I remember it was originally his. We both enjoy adventure in life but temper it with a large dose of practicality. And neither of us believes that any real work is accomplished unless a decent sweat is broken.

I watch him now and wonder if I will approach my own mortality with the same grace and courage he has shown in the past months against his cancer.

We land in Phoenix and wait for the other passengers to file out of the plane before attempting to disembark ourselves. A new skycap loads Dad into another wheelchair and takes us to the next gate.

More waiting provides Dad another opportunity to use the restroom. Until the cancer, my father was healthy and robust, a farmer who tended livestock, hoisted bags of seed corn, and scampered beneath tractors and combines to perform surgical repairs. I can only imagine the embarrassment he now feels to have his daughter wait for him with a wheelchair outside the restroom door.

Dad and I return to Mom who notes the different fashions and hairstyles of the passengers.

"I remember when people got dressed up to go on a plane. They cared about how they looked," she reminisces. "It was a thing of pride."

While she is still speaking, Dad and I simultaneously whiff the scent of a hot dog. Neither of us particularly likes this food at home, but today the savory smell wakes both of our appetites.

Food has always been one of Dad's life pleasures. His favorite ice cream is "cold," and he claims he never met a pie he wouldn't eat. If Mom made a dessert to take to a social function, it always arrived with a corner missing where Dad had taken a sample.

"You wouldn't want to serve bad brownies to your friends, would you?" he defended himself.

Dinner was always ready and consumed at noon but supper might be kept warm in the oven long after the sun went down during spring planting or autumn harvest days. Unless it was unavoidable, Dad never missed a meal.

Now the chemotherapy affects the flavor of his food, even the taste of the water. He describes it as a metallic linger. As long as he takes these drugs, he eats for the nutritional and fuel value only, no longer for the enjoyment of something sweet, cold, and creamy melting on his tongue.

When the hot dog scent rouses his appetite, I am determined to find one for him. I search the terminal corridor, but no vendor is in site. Maybe the waft of the food came from a traveler passing through from an adjacent terminal.

"There's a Burger King just down a ways," I offer to Dad. "Or I could check out the next terminal."

"Nah, that's okay," he says. His craving has passed.

We repeat the plane loading, safety drills, and in-flight entertainment from the last leg of the trip. I brought five books for the three of us to read throughout this week. Dad prefers a James Michener epic or a *Wallace's Farmer* magazine to my selection, but I doubt if he would read even those today.

I begin reading a novel about a boy with Asperger's, a type of autism. The character makes an astute observation about the difference between a dog with a broken leg and a person with the same injury. Without consideration for its injuries, the dog jumps and runs the day after the break because the animal doesn't know that the activity might trigger more pain. A human, on the other hand, is anxious about even the smallest of movements, adjusting his injured limb only when absolutely necessary to avoid even the possibility of further agony.

This excerpt from the book perfectly describes my father in his current condition. Dad dreads every bump, rough floor, and uneven surface of this trip. The potential for anguish exists each time we enter and exit the car, sit down or stand up from a chair, or move past any other person in close proximity. If Dad isn't feeling the pain, he is anticipating it.

At Salt Lake City, again we are the last ones off. A tall, twenty-something skycap waits for us on the landing where the jet bridge connects to the plane. Although polite, he seems to be on a schedule and handles Dad like a sack of seed corn. As soon as Dad sits in the wheelchair, the skycap bolts toward the baggage claim. Our airport chauffer has no concept that the rough ride is wreaking havoc with Dad's leg, or that my mother is literally running to keep up with them. Under the weight of our carry-on bags, I also struggle to keep the pace.

The impatient skycap waits for me to retrieve both pieces of checked luggage from the carousel, anxious to receive his tip and meet another arrival.

"Do you know where the car rental area is?" I ask. Rather than answer my question, he spins Dad's chair around and charges through the airport exit. Mom and I continue the chase, this time through a maze of ground transportation options. The skycap comes to a startling halt directly in front of the rental car concessions.

"Thank you so much," Mom says to the race-chair driver and tips him with two dollars of loose change from her pocket. "I don't think we could have found this place without you."

A middle-aged clerk with a British accent greets us from underneath the green Alamo sign. While she searches for our reservation on her computer, Dad paces the long room to circulate the blood in his legs.

"How many drivers?" the agent asks.

"Just one," I say quietly. "Just me."

Mom, standing next to me, doesn't say a word. Her raised eyebrows make the statement for her.

"Okay. For just another $20 a day you can upgrade to a larger model," the agent informs us. "Would you like to do that today?"

The brand of vehicle doesn't influence me, but I wonder if a larger car might have more legroom for Dad than the Buick currently assigned to us. Nodding in Dad's direction, I explain the need for extra space to the agent.

"My own father has the same difficulty," she sympathizes. "And actually, there is more legroom in the LeSabre than the larger car so you should stick with this one."

I thank her for her expertise as she rips the computer-generated contract from the printer.

"To get to the car, you just walk out these two doors here," she points behind her. As she looks up she sees Dad still gimping around the corridor.

"You know, just wait here. I'll bring the car to you."

In the same time it takes Dad to reach the Alamo exit, the agent has retrieved and delivered to us our forest green chariot with tan interior. I load our bags into the trunk while Mom experiences another exhausting episode loading Dad. When Dad finally settles in the front passenger seat, Mom folds the walker and keeps it in the backseat next to her.

"Don't you want that in the trunk, Mom?"

"No, it's fine here." Perhaps it is reassuring for her to keep it close.

I adjust my mirrors and head toward the interstate.

"You should have heard that girl in there, Charles. She was trying to get us to take the higher-priced car, but we weren't buying it, were we, Rin."

Mom's impression of the car rental transaction catches me off guard. While I thought the agent went out of her way to steer us to the right-sized car, Mom believed the woman was trying to sell us unwanted luxury in the form of a larger car.

"She must have thought we were green. I don't need that kind of car. She was really pushing for it, wasn't she?"

I add communication difficulties to the list of unanticipated challenges to face on this trip.

We begin driving north toward Idaho Falls, Idaho, where we will stay tonight. As I begin driving in unfamiliar territory, I realize I need another person to navigate. I offer the maps to Dad, but he's too tired and waves them off to Mom sitting behind him. I'm not entirely comfortable having exits and junctions called out from the backseat, the worst location from which to see the road signs and markings, but we have no other option.

One of my favorite travel pastimes is the license-plate game. In this diversion, players search for one vehicle license from each state. Hawaii and Rhode Island are highly prized, as are U.S. territories such as Guam or Puerto Rico. Although resistant, my own kids are required to play along to pacify me on any car trip over two hours. I propose it now to my parents, if for no other reason than to make the time pass more quickly.

"Oh, this will be fun," Dad says sarcastically.

"Lookit." I encourage them. "Already I see Utah, Montana, and Idaho." With the enthusiasm of an underpaid scribe, Mom logs the names of these states on a yellow legal pad I stuck in my bag in case we needed to write notes or play the license-plate game.

By three o'clock Iowa time, my stomach growls for lunch. "Are you ready to stop yet, Dad? Anything look good to you?"

"Nah, I'm not particularly hungry. Just stop anywhere," Dad answers.

I know my father well enough to know that he doesn't really mean he would eat *anywhere*. He wants a local diner that serves meat loaf with mashed potatoes and gravy.

After passing a string of fast food restaurants in Salt Lake City, we finally cross into Idaho. From the interstate we spy a well-kept restaurant painted white with black trim.

"How about this for a place to stop?"

Neither of them objects as I take the exit ramp and enter a much slower-paced world. I park in the space marked with a wheelchair stencil, and Mom pulls the universally recognized blue handicapped parking tag from her purse. I leave it swinging from the rearview mirror as I retrieve Dad's walker from the seat behind me.

Inside the roadside café we are greeted with red plaid tablecloths, plastic autumn flowers, and Halloween decorations on the walls. Local residents drink coffee and eat pie at the dozen or so tables in the dining room. A waitress in her midfifties brings us menus and informs us that the special of the day is a hot Philly sandwich with a side of chili.

Dad skips the menu and orders the special. Mom does the same, only she adds fries. Normally, Mom never consumes this much food, and Dad hasn't had an appetite since starting the chemo. I order a small salad, assuming that when we reach the hotel, we'll have something more substantial.

We study the pictures on the walls and take turns using the bathrooms. Lunch arrives in less than ten minutes, but it's too late for Dad whose appetite has already waned. He eats two spoonfuls of the chili and a bite of the sandwich. His thirst continues, though, and he pours the water from Mom's glass into his own.

"Wrap that up, Ma," he points to his sandwich, "and save it for me for later."

Mom, on the other hand, devours everything she ordered. She didn't even offer me a French fry.

As we walk out of the restaurant, I notice a beautiful array of pink roses climbing the trellis in front of the building. I think it would make a nice background for a photograph of Mom and Dad.

"Hey, go stand in front of the flowers over there," I suggest. "I'll take a picture. I'll take one with your camera, too."

"What camera?" Dad asks. "We didn't bring a camera."

"Why would we?" Mom shares his sentiment. "We only look at the pictures once after they are developed, and then they go into a box."

"Yeah," Dad continues, "plus they have no meaning to anyone but us."

Apparently, my parents have reached a point in their lives where they no longer need or want new photographs, not even of each other. Given Dad's tenuous health, I'm more anxious than ever to have a good photograph of my parents together.

"Humor me."

I snap the picture and drop my camera into my purse. After Dad inches back into the car, I merge onto the interstate highway without any further discussion of photographs or memories.

Idaho Falls is not a random stop in our itinerary. As we made plans for this trip, Mom reminded me that her own mother spent part of her childhood near this town. Old diaries of my grandmother included brief notes about their Idaho settlement. Mom even found an early 1900s postcard of Idaho Falls showing Broadway Street, with a trestle bridge spanning the Snake River. As we would be so close, Mom suggested that it might be nice to at least drive through the town, and I thought it would be even better if we spent the night here.

The Comfort Inn Hotel in Idaho Falls is easy to find. Dad stays in the car but gives directions for Mom and me to investigate the floor plan.

"If the room is too far away for me to walk, find a different room. Or a different hotel if necessary."

The clerk informs us that the room is further down the hall than Dad will want, but we reason that he might actually appreciate the chance to stretch his legs. I fill out the registration card at the front desk.

We return to the car ready to unpack, but Dad has another idea.

"I want to see the town. Let's go take a look at it before I get out of the car for the night."

Mom and I climb back into the car and drive across the river into the town. We tour past brick storefronts, comfortable houses with decent-sized front lawns, and parks with both children and adults playing in them. Each of us sees a business that piques our individual interests—a fabric store for Mom, a farm co-op for Dad, and for me, a yarn shop that displays a wonderful palette of colors through the large window framing thousands of skeins inside.

"I could retire to a little town like this," Dad says. "Just right for me."

The short drive is enough to satisfy our curiosity, and we return to the hotel, to our single room with two double beds.

"Mom, do you want to sleep with me?" I offer to Mom knowing that she is protective of Dad's leg even in sleep.

"Oh, no. That's no problem. He doesn't move around much with his leg as it is. I'll just sleep here." She pats the left side of the bed where Dad is already laying.

Dad naps while Mom searches her luggage for medicine. The clock reads six o'clock, and the notion of dinner seems to have disappeared from the list of things to do tonight. I spied an indoor pool when we checked in. After I dig my swimming suit out of my suitcase, I leave to find a little privacy and to give the same to my parents.

Melting into the luxury of solitude, the tension of my mind and body drift away in the chlorinated water. Only when another swimmer enters the pool do I leave my private spa.

Water still drips from my hair and onto the carpet as I open the door of our room. Mom is reading a book and Dad is in the same place as when I left. His eyes are closed, but he is awake, humming a tune and rocking his left foot in rhythm. Dad used to nap this same way on the living room sofa each day after lunch, offering one shiny penny to any of us kids who were willing to comb his hair. His respites only lasted ten or twenty minutes, long enough to recharge him for the rest of the day. He seems to require a lot more sleep lately.

I rinse off in the shower and put on my pajamas. While I am tired, I'm not very sleepy. I think I'll knit for a while.

I learned to knit when I was in high school but forgot how much I enjoyed it until a friend reignited my interest a few years ago. Selecting new yarns, trying different colors and textures is a favorite part of any project. Even so, I equally enjoy the soothing and familiar sound of the repetitive click of the needles. Stitch after deliberate stitch, without any short cut or technological timesaving device, I find great solace in the slow, methodical movement toward my finished creation.

Inside one of my suitcases hides a silk-wool blend of yarn. After I burrow inside to find it, I begin knitting Christmas gifts for Elisabeth and Clarissa, a scarf and matching mittens for each of my daughters.

After only three rows, I realize my family, back on Central Standard Time, is also ready to climb into bed. Although "HOME" is programmed into my cell phone, I prefer to punch the individual digits and wait for someone to answer.

Elisabeth picks up the phone, and I have a one-sided conversation with her.

"How was your day?"

"What did you do?"

"Have you brushed your teeth?"

"Did you tell your father to pick you up tomorrow?"

"Do you need lunch money?"

"Did you pay your band fees?"

"Do you have early practice?"

I repeat nearly every word to Clare and Eric when the phone passes to them. Mom and Dad laugh as I attempt to parent from a thousand miles away. Even though Rob perfectly manages all of these details, I miss being with them. I even talk to Daisy, our Shetland sheepdog, before saying good night.

Dad is now ready for serious sleeping as opposed to simply napping. After he finishes in the bathroom, he takes off his plaid shirt but leaves on his white T-shirt for pajamas. He backs up to the edge of the bed until he feels it next to his leg. Then he sits down slowly. Mom, with her hair wrapped in a scarf, unties and removes his shoes and socks with the same gentleness she demonstrated last night. Dad shakes his trousers onto the floor without actually standing.

When he is ready, he scoots as far into the middle of the bed as he can before tipping backward onto the mattress. The momentum of the fall allows his legs to swing up and onto the bed where he makes a few adjustments. Mom places a towel under his right leg as a final touch.

I switch off the lights and climb into my own bed with much less drama. Dad moans when he shifts his weight just to make noise. Very quickly, his uniform breathing signals he's already back to sleep.

My own eyes continue to stare into the darkness. This day has gone better than I imagined when I saw Dad twenty-four hours ago. Still, we have to repeat this day seven more times.

I take a deep breath before falling asleep myself.

Thursday

September 29

During our review of the town last night, we crossed the Snake River, and I noticed a walking path that ran parallel with the water.

"I'm going to walk on that trail we saw yesterday," I say to Mom and Dad before they're even out of bed.

"Well, you be careful," Mom warns me first, but Dad also chimes in.

"Yeah, all kinds of freaks are out there."

With plenty of light at seven o'clock and three gray-haired ladies ahead of me, I feel quite safe on this trail. Still, I quickly walk three miles and head back to the Comfort Inn before Mom and Dad can start to worry.

Just after I return to the room and close the door behind me, Dad explodes one of his primal belches.

"Dad!" I protest. "The people in the next room will wonder what kind of animal is hibernating in here."

"What?" he asks innocently. I roll my eyes at him.

"Let's go get breakfast," I say, hinting that we haven't eaten since our late lunch yesterday. "It's free."

This hotel chain was created exactly for people like my parents—clean, moderately priced, and breakfast included.

Forward progress down the hall is slow and deliberate. Dad steps out with his left foot. Then, with most of his weight pressing down on the walker, he drags his right foot to catch up. He creates his own cadence: lift-down-limp, lift-down-limp. Mom and I guard him on either side, protecting him from others or from a fall.

At the lobby-turned-dining room, Dad eases himself onto a chair before directing Mom to bring him some breakfast.

"Get me some eggs and a waffle, will ya."

Mom fills a plate for Dad but takes nothing for herself. Breakfast usually doesn't agree with Mom. The food quarrels with her digestion.

Dad only tolerates three small bites before he reaches his limit. Mom leans over to eat a few more bites of his eggs. She would rather have an upset stomach than waste the food.

My own gurgling stomach embarrasses me in light of my parents' lack of appetite. When the cold milk splashes against the pit of my stomach, I remember again that we only ate one meal yesterday. Any guilty feelings disappear with my toast.

By the time we return to the room, Dad needs to rest again. He also desires privacy in the bathroom.

"The car needs filling up." My statement is truthful as well as an excuse to leave Dad alone. "You want to come with me, Mom?"

She needs no persuading, and we set out on a search for fuel. As we pass through the lobby, I deposit Eric's birthday card at the front desk. I probably care more about it being late than he does.

A gas station sits kitty-corner from the hotel. I fill the tank until it can hold no more and pay with cash that Dad gave me before we left the room. Neither Mom nor I are ready to return immediately to our room, so I propose an alternative.

When I was walking this morning, I passed an old monument where the original bridge crossed the Snake River. I describe the marker to Mom. "Maybe it's the same bridge you showed me on Grandma's postcard."

Mom is kindled by the prospect of sharing a piece of her own mother's history. We drive to the same parking lot I used this morning and walk the short distance to the large stone memorial. Both of us are convinced this is the same location depicted on the old card.

"Do you want me to take a picture of you next to the marker?" I ask her.

Now Mom is grateful that I brought my camera. She wants to brag to her sister about finding the monument and bridge.

When we return to the hotel, Dad is ready for the road and to fulfill his long-time dream of seeing the Grand Teton mountain range. I take our bags to the lobby and check out while Dad walks the distance to the car. We both reach the Buick at the same time.

"Maybe I could drive for a little bit," Dad suggests.

I've deliberately avoided this conversation, hoping that he wouldn't notice I was always the one behind the wheel. Now I have to justify my reasons for keeping him in the passenger seat.

"You need to be able to enjoy all the scenery," I say, which is partially true. "It's okay. You can leave all the driving to me."

"Well, it would actually be easier for me to get in and out of the car if I was driving," he says with reproach.

Mom says nothing, which only adds to the tension.

"You can't, Dad," I say respectfully. "I didn't put your name on the car rental agreement."

In silence that speaks every word, Dad proceeds to the passenger side of the car and executes the tedious entry procedures with extra flourish for my benefit. Mom assists him as I place his walker in the backseat. I slide into the driver's seat, start the car, and leave the hotel without either of us revisiting the subject.

We head northwest toward the mountains. As we leave the city limits, I accelerate, anxious to explore the landscape before us.

"Slow down! Slow down!" Dad yells.

No obstacles clutter the road ahead of us, and my speedometer reads well below the speed limit. Still, I check my rear-view mirror for flashing lights.

"What? What's wrong?" I look back at Mom for clues.

"I want to look at all of these tractors lined up here ready to sell." Dad calmly points out his window to the bright, shiny agricultural equipment aligned in neat rows.

I remember his admonition to stop at every farm implement dealer along the way.

"Do you want me to pull over?"

"No, just slow down. But if I was driving we would have stopped." He raises his eyebrows at me to emphasize his point.

I glare back at him.

"Well, I would have," he says.

U.S. Highway 26 is a two-lane road winding through eastern Idaho. After a series of name changes, it will take us directly to Jackson, Wyoming. Just as Dad requested, we drive on as many back roads as we can find.

The details of the autumn vegetation are so much more defined from this distance than from the interstate. Embroidered on the hills before us are faded greens, sharp oranges, brilliant reds, and dusty golds. Knots of purple and brown weave up and down the valley. Together, the texture and hues create a heathery yarn I wish I could knit.

With each passing acre, the three of us attempt to identify the crops in the field. We presume they are potatoes because we are, after all, in Idaho, but their appearance seems different from those we grow at home in the garden.

"I can't tell what it is," Dad says, "because I can't get a chance to look at it for very long." I'm speeding along at fifty-eight miles per hour.

"We can stop if you like."

"No, but if I was driving ..." He trails off purposefully.

Less than five hundred feet ahead of us is a dirt road leading deeper into the fields. I turn the corner safely but sharp enough to stir up the dust, stopping directly in front of a yellow, dusty crop waiting to be harvested.

"Okay, Dad. Here you go."

"You didn't have to stop here," he says apologetically.

Regardless of my motivation, we now have an unobstructed view of the vegetation. We crinkle our foreheads and examine the brown spindly stems emerging from the soil. My parents discourage my offer to swipe a vine out of the ground to have a closer look. Through the LeSabre's windshield, all three agree that these are, in fact, potato paddocks.

In the heart of the Loess Hills of western Iowa, my parents' farm is as fertile as any can be, dense, thick, and tillable deeper than they make the plows. The rich, aromatic, dark soil packs together if squeezed between my fingers but crumbles away when I release my grip. With the help of the hot and humid Iowa weather, plants thrive in its embrace.

Dad has lived on this farm most of his life, born in the same house where he raised his own children. About a third of the farmland is timber and pasture, while the remaining acres are planted in traditional Midwestern crops of oats, corn, alfalfa, and beans. Or at least it was until about ten years ago when Mom and Dad placed the majority of the farm into a government conservation program.

My parents bought the main parcel from Dad's parents who farmed it during the depression of the 1930s. Like many others at the time, my grandparents reached a point when they could no longer afford the mortgage payments. In disgrace, Grandpa walked to the bank in Council Bluffs and handed the deed over to his creditor.

"Charlie," the banker said to my grandfather, also named Charles. "I don't need any more farms. I have a hundred of them stacked up here already," he said, pointing to a pile of foreclosure papers. "Please. Please, go back and try again."

With new resolve, Grandpa returned to the farm. He and his family were ultimately able to turn their financial crisis around, but progress was slow, and their success was not without tears or sacrifice. One spring tornado ripped through the farm, bending corncribs, killing livestock, and tearing walls from the house. The barn and grain bins that survived the storm remained functional but permanently disfigured with a forty-five-degree lean to the east. My sisters and I had to conform to the same angle when we slipped inside the twisted crib doorway to gather corncobs for the wood stove.

Financial hardship and unpredictable weather were insignificant compared to the human tragedy that came upon the family. On a sun-scorched Thursday in July, my grandfather promised his two younger sons that if they finished laying down the corn, he would take them fishing. My father and his older brother, Lester, worked hard in the morning and early afternoon for the chance to feel the cool water before sunset.

Dad wasn't quite fourteen, and Lester had just graduated from high school. One of their sisters, Mabel, lived in Council Bluffs with her husband, George, and their two small daughters, one of them still too young to say "Daddy."

When the chores were finished, Grandpa and the boys left my Grandma Bessie with Mabel for the rest of the afternoon. George went with the farm crew to Lake Manawa, a large lake on the south side of Council Bluffs known for both fishing and swimming.

The four began to fish on the south side of the lake, near an old, mostly abandoned beach. Wanting to improve his chances of a catch, Lester waded out onto a sand bar. Without warning, the lake floor dropped and swallowed him into fifteen feet of water.

Whether he disregarded the danger to his own life or merely acted out of instinct, brother-in-law George immediately dived in after Lester. The pull of the whirlpool was too great, though, and the water encircled him as well.

With the adrenaline and energy of the moment, my own father tried to follow the other two. Grandpa recognized the precariousness of the situation and forced his youngest son back from the death hole, knowing that in doing so, he was sacrificing his other son and son-in-law.

George's body was found twenty minutes later, but rescue crews had to use draglines to locate Lester. In agony, the surviving father and brother watched helplessly, staring into the continuous deep and churning water.

The sun was growing low in the sky, and Grandpa and Dad needed to get back to Grandma and Mabel. They were further delayed by a stop at the hospital for Dad. When he stepped out after Lester, he gashed his foot on some stone pilings and now required stitches in his foot. His right foot.

When Grandpa and Dad finally returned, Grandpa recited what had happened and why George and Lester were not with them. The darkness of that night enveloped them all.

The family spent the following days, weeks, and years trying to regain their balance, each of them devastated by the impact of their individual losses.

Every July, my father and Aunt Mabel talk on the phone and without explanation or detail, remember together what happened that summer day. Recently, Dad confided to her that he felt so alone during that time, not only for the loss of his older brother, but because no one consoled him. Friends, neighbors, and family swarmed around my grandparents and Aunt Mabel with her two fatherless children, but no one knew how to comfort the thirteen-year-old who would carry this nightmare the rest of his life. Instead, he spent long hours sitting on the edge of the porch quietly passing his hand over the neck of the family dog, stroke after stroke, trying to make the scene from the lake disappear from his mind.

Mabel was forced to move back to the farm where Grandma and Grandpa could help her raise the girls. For the rest of her life, Grandma Bessie could not speak Lester's name without tears welling up in her eyes.

As tragic as it was for my grandmother, aunt, and father, the hell was magnified for my grandfather. He was powerless in the face of the drownings and could never extinguish the agonizing sights, smells or sounds from his memory. Grandpa sobbed for months, unable to recover and compose himself. Lacking both strength and desire to return to the daily routine and details of farming, he was virtually paralyzed.

As Dad had finished the eighth grade in May and was physically strong enough to assume responsibilities for the animals and crops, he took over many of the daily farm chores when Grandpa could not. Maybe Dad would have taken up farming eventually, but the events of that summer day forever sealed his future. My father never returned to high school but instead began his life as a farmer.

My parents and I are comfortable, even relaxed in the familiarity of row crops and agricultural machinery—monster contraptions that unearth and capture bushels of produce. As if writing a final exam in college, we compare and contrast these machines with those used for corn and beans, identify the other crops ready for their Idaho harvest, and estimate the price of a good piece of farmland in the area. The fascination with these fields distracts Dad from both the discomfort in his leg and the fact that he's not driving.

As we travel further through the valley, alongside the gentle but deep streams, the scene changes from harvest fields to grazing pastures. Ultimately the autumn foliage welcomes us into the mountain pass.

"This is beautiful country, all right," Dad says, paying his respect.

"It just needs a little snow on those tips to really set it off," Mom adds.

Just after the pass, we intersect with Jackson, a town that serves skiing as well as other tourist interests of the Tetons.

"Do you want to get out and look around here a little, Dad?" It's been about three hours since we left Idaho Falls, and I want him to walk as much as possible.

"Nah, I don't see any implement dealers here. Let's go on."

We head north into Grand Teton National Park, watching the mountains swell in size and detail. Craggy peaks and canyon folds stand in stark contrast to the lush green of the lodge pole pine trees and meadowland floor. No foothills announce the majesty of the mountains, only the bold statement of the steel gray sedimentary rock.

The Moose Visitor Center, the park's headquarters, sits just inside the Tetons' south border.

"I need a break," declares Dad.

We turn into the lot and use the parking spot directly in front of the entrance to the visitor center. Once inside, Dad immediately uses the bathroom while Mom and I look around.

A giant three-dimensional bas-relief map of the park stands in the center of the room. Dad joins us and begins to study the details of the map. I step away from my parents to approach the park ranger standing behind a long counter. He is dressed in a sage green uniform with coordinating tie.

"I'm wondering if you can suggest a driving tour. I need something that will allow us to see a lot of the park but doesn't require very much walking."

The brief silence and glaring eyes of the ranger reveal his scorn for this tourist before him who seeks to explore such a treasure of nature without ever stepping foot onto the grass.

"I'm traveling with my parents," I explain, nodding toward Mom and Dad. "They really want to see the park, but my father isn't able to walk on uneven surfaces." Much less any other surface, I think to myself.

The ranger watches Dad who is bent over his walker but whose face beams up into the eyes of an eight-foot grizzly bear. The bear's menacing grin frightens visitors as it stands on its hind legs with front claws poised to strike. Dad drinks it all in and looks around for more.

"If you stay on the main road," the ranger refocuses his attention and directs me to the map on the countertop in front of him, "really, you'll be able to see quite a bit." The ranger even sounds sympathetic now.

After we finish admiring the raised maps and stuffed bears, we forage for our own lunch at a general store adjacent to the visitor's center. Kerosene oil is for sale in one aisle and gourmet ice cream in the next. Mom and I purchase three soft-bread sandwiches from the deli, a bag of pretzels, and a diet pop for me. A roadside pullout is just across the road, and it's there that we choose to eat our lunch. We may be inside the car, but we have a spectacular view of the mountains over the dashboard.

"That reminds me," Mom says between bites of egg salad, "I was supposed to call Cynthia." I don't make the connection between this magnificent scene and Mom's thought to call her youngest child, but I don't ask.

Last spring, Cyn bought Mom and Dad a cell phone. Dad doesn't even know how to turn it on, but Mom, who taught herself how to use her personal computer and navigate the worldwide web, owns a nicer cell phone than me. Not that I carry anything very technologically advanced.

Today's communication devices are a lifetime away from the party-line system we used in the 1960s. Before we rotary dialed our call to a four-digit number, we had to first listen for the mechanical buzz in the earpiece in case one of the neighbors was already using the line. I still wait for a dial tone before making a call.

"Well, we're here," Mom tells Cyn, sounding slightly surprised that we've made it this far.

Cyn visits the farm often, bringing her husband Brad and their two-year-old son, Keasen, with her. Keasen doesn't realize it, of course, but he is a rare source of brightness in the difficult days of Dad's cancer. He doesn't need much encouragement to dance in the middle of the living room. Dad, with both legs propped up in his recliner, keeps time with his left foot and thrives on the entertainment. Cynthia stands guard, worried that her toddler will spin around one time too often, and in his dizziness, trip and fall onto Grandpa's sore leg.

"I just wanted to test the signal and make sure we could reach you," Mom says into the phone.

I suspect the phone call was more about missing Cyn than wanting to test the limits of her cell phone plan.

Mom and Dad eat only part of their lunch. As they did yesterday, they wrap up the leftovers and save them for an appetite that will never surface. As I did earlier today with the Philly sandwiches, I'll throw them away later.

At thirty-five miles per hour, we have the luxury of watching the sky change shape and color over the mountains. Our eyes drink in the textures of the hills as we keep watch for wildlife. So far, all mountain creatures have evaded us.

Dad's fever, though, has not. If anything, his temperature is higher than it was this morning. He turns up the heat in the car to ward off his chills. The warm air smothers me in the front seat as he falls asleep for an afternoon nap. In the hot, dry car with no conversation or wildlife to entertain me, I grow drowsy myself.

As I wriggle out of my coat, I can hear Dad snoring. I take advantage of his semiconscious state to switch the temperature over to the blue side. Ten minutes later and ten degrees cooler, Dad wakes up shivering. He reaches across the control panel to make the climate in the car red again.

We battle over the thermostat in this way until we reach the Jenny Lake Overlook. When Rob and I were here with the kids, I thought this was one of the most beautiful views in the area. The crystal blue lake reflects the steel gray mountains, an image that could have been, and often is, used in a National Geographic calendar. Even though Dad doesn't feel well, he came here to see just this sort of thing. I'm determined that the sight of this lake will be worth the trouble of dragging him out of the car.

As predicted, Dad has trouble with the five steps from the parking lot to the overlook. It doesn't help that we are overrun by a busload of senior citizens in search of animal pelts displayed at the far end of the path. Several others hurry to the lecture given by one of the park rangers regarding the geological make-up of the region.

Like a mirror, the deep water reflects the grandeur of the mountain scenery, just as I remembered. The pine trees meet the edge of the lake on the north side, and variegated brown, green, and gray vegetation grows on the opposite side. As the hills climb higher, they become more jagged until the sharp peaks pierce the cloudless, brilliant blue sky. The mountain and lake provide a perfect backdrop for another photograph of my parents.

"Hey, let me take your picture here," I suggest, even though Dad clearly is not in a mood for photographs.

With his blue denim shirt partially untucked at his waist, he and Mom pause in front of a pile of rocks strategically placed to prevent tourists from a plunge over the edge. Unfortunately, the afternoon sun filters through the trees and shadows the faces of my parents. I don't want to ask Dad to shift to the left just so I can snap a decent photo for this year's Christmas card.

"Let me try moving over here." I try a new spot, but the angle is no better and quite possibly worse. Finally, I just click off three photos and jam the camera back into my purse.

Dad does appreciate the scenery, but his pain taints any lingering enjoyment. His only desire is to return to the car, locate the hotel, and retire for the night.

We have daylight for almost another hour, and Coulter Bay, one of the park's larger campgrounds, is only a little further north of our hotel. The road follows the lake edge, giving Dad a closer opportunity to see the mountain water. He doesn't know it yet, but he's going to like this side trip. I turn left at the Coulter Bay Village entrance.

In the summer, this park packs in the campers. By the end of September, only a few stragglers remain. This particular site, complete with a ranger station, picnic and camping area, dining room, gas station, store, stables, cabins, and marina, is closed for the season. Although it is ghost-town eerie, the absence of people and traffic allows us to steer into tight spaces that would otherwise be inaccessible. I'm also free to drive slowly throughout the park without worrying about vehicles lining up behind me.

Our review of Coulter Bay lasts only a few minutes before we start back toward the main highway. As we are about to leave, two mule deer stand frozen in the grass to our left.

"Hey, hey! What's that?" I'm more enthusiastic than most might be when seeing these deer. Such animals are not the exotic species one conjures up when contemplating grand national parks, but because the only other wild kingdom affiliate we saw today was a stuffed bear, it satisfies us enough.

Mom and Dad's fiftieth wedding anniversary is this coming May. To help them celebrate, my siblings and I want to give our parents one night on this trip by themselves. I admit I will benefit from this arrangement as well.

In August, when I called the Jackson Lake Lodge for reservations, all the main lodge rooms were already reserved.

"You might ask about cancellations when you get here. Sometimes we get a few of those. You just never know." The woman on the other end of the line tried to give me hope as she booked us into an unremarkable cabin.

I cross my fingers a special room will be available as Mom and I enter the dark paneled lobby this late afternoon.

"Well, we don't have anything for tonight," offers one of the clerks checking us in.

"Do any of the cottages have a view of the mountains?" I ask as a back-up.

"No. Sorry. None of those left either."

Mom and Dad weren't expecting a private room for tonight so they won't be disappointed. I feel badly, though, that our plan to give them even one night of luxury is a bust.

"Okay. Well, I need a room that doesn't have any steps, or at least not very many." I explain Dad's disability to all three clerks standing behind the high counter, and they begin to search.

"There is a duplex at the very back of the lot," says the first clerk. "It has a curb, but a handicapped room is right next door, so there should be a ramp fairly close by."

"Okay. We'll try that," I say. "Also, do you have a wheelchair we can borrow for tonight? We have reservations for dinner at the lodge."

"Yes, we do," responds a second clerk. "We'll have it delivered down to you at your cabin."

She notes the time of our dinner reservation, and Mom and I return to Dad waiting in the car. The distance from the lodge to our duplex is less than two blocks, but I drive to save Dad the walk. He navigates the landscape successfully while I haul the luggage and coats inside to Room 500J.

A kitchen galley sits immediately to our left. The main room opens up straight ahead with two double beds and a writing desk. Large windows line the wall opposite the front door. Even though it must be the same size as our hotel room last night, the vaulted ceiling gives the illusion of a more expansive space and certainly more character. A door next to Mom and Dad's bed leads to a small patio outside.

Once in the room, Dad immediately turns up the thermostat and asks Mom to find extra blankets. He lays his swollen ankle and tired leg on the bed and falls asleep on top of the bedspread. Mom discovers a wool blanket in one of the dresser drawers and unfolds it to cover him. I toss off my coat as well as my sweater to avoid further perspiration.

The wood stove at the farm provides a type of heat that is direct, instant, and penetrating. It is also difficult to control. The only way to regulate the temperature is to open outdoor windows or doors to cold rooms. Mom and Dad are used to temperatures hovering at eighty degrees and are never warm enough when they visit any of their children. When we visit them, we remember to dress in layers to avoid wilting in the heat.

The first stove I remember from my childhood stood four feet tall. Round, black, and balanced on claw feet, its windows were made of thin mica sheeting that allowed us to see the flames inside. Dad pulled up his oak rocking chair in front of the grimy potbellied stove as the fire snapped. When we stood on the rockers, Dad fed us butter brickle ice cream scooped from a gallon container with a fork. The tines of the fork gave better traction in the deep frozen ice cream than a spoon. Occasionally, one of us would slip off and our toes were smashed between the rocker and floor. Dad coaxed us back on, making our tears disappear with another forkful of ice cream.

The stove worked overtime to heat the old drafty house that was my father's actual birthplace. By the 1970s, Mom and Dad were tired of the slanting floors, sagging ceilings, and rotting walls. They drew up plans and built a ranch replacement less than fifty feet west of the old structure. The modern house was sturdy, functional, contained no lead-based paint, and possessed no character or charm whatsoever.

With the new house came a new wood stove, an uninspired brown metal rectangle model. The pudgy black stove was relegated to the basement along with the strong wooden rocker. Eventually, the rocker came to live at my house, and the old potbellied stove now warms Dad's wood shop. Both are useful again.

After twenty-five years, the rectangle gave out and was replaced by another black stove that included some of the old-fashioned features. Dad wakes up through the night to "feed the dragon," as Mom says, and keep the fire burning. They did install a water heat system in case there comes a time when they can no longer cut, stack, and carry the heavy logs for the fire. For now, my parents continue to soak up the intense heat of their wood stove, more comforting than ever when keeping away the chills of Dad's illness.

The temperatures in this Teton bungalow are too warm for me to think, and I escape to cooler air through the back door, past my sleeping father. An Adirondack chair in the lawn behind the duplex serves as my late-afternoon base from which I make contact with home.

Rob reports that the world I left in Iowa revolves fairly well without me. Even though I'm the only one who wanted to go, my family will attend the violin concert tonight. Before they leave, Rob passes the phone to each of my children as I convey what will be unused parenting tips for the next day.

Our dinner reservations tonight are for the Mural Room inside the main lodge, timed to coincide with the sun melting behind the mountains. My parents will have a spectacular view, elegant food, and an amorous setting, even if their daughter is in tow.

"Is this dinner thing somethin' we gotta do?" Dad bursts my romantic bubble. "I mean, do we have reservations and whatnot, or is it just a walk-in type deal?"

He hurts. He's tired. He doesn't want to leave this sauna. I convince myself that he's not deliberately sabotaging the evening.

"Yes. We have reservations," I say, using my finish-your-homework tone of voice. "It's part of an anniversary gift to you and Mom from your four kids." I add this last part, hoping that the financial arrangement will sweeten the deal for him.

"Humph." Dad's feelings about the evening are clear. "I'll bet you ten bucks your mother doesn't order much of anything. She eats like a bird. She certainly won't eat any meat."

"Come on, Dad."

He grunts to let me know that he thinks this dinner is an extremely foolish idea. I propose a compromise.

"Okay, how about after tonight, we'll just eat a good lunch and then not worry about dinner?" I wanted to bargain for at least one full meal a day.

"Sounds like a con-founded good idea to me," Dad replies in a vernacular that only he uses and only his family understands.

A knock at our door announces the arrival of Dad's transportation. A mustached man dressed in a black cowboy outfit stands at the door, behind the chair. My gaze lasts just a brief moment while I assess whether he is for real or if his attire is part of the hotel ambience. Either way, he leaves without offering any assistance to the restaurant.

Mom and I guide Dad into the chair, out the door, and onto the sidewalk. Unfortunately, the walking path has significant cracks between the concrete squares. The wheels of the chair catch on each gap, and Dad jolts back and forth.

"Move over here, Rin." Dad wants off the sidewalk and onto the paved parking area. I comply, but the parking surface isn't much better. The paving is pocked with holes and asphalt patches. Each pass over a seam or divot is like a knife in the back of his leg.

We find a place in the road with a smoother surface, making it easier on both Dad and myself. Dad uses the opportunity to pour out a belch, not a hiccup or an air bubble, but a fierce storm from the bottom of his belly.

"Dad!"

"Sorry," he says, again innocently.

"Dad, does your medication make you do that?" Not that this is a change from his precancer behavior.

"Nah, it's just natural," he says.

"Well, at least keep your lips closed," I plead for the sake of my mother.

"If I do that," he explains logically, "all of that pressure would build up and explode."

Inside the Grand Teton Lodge, we take the elevator to the upper lobby, a large room paneled with dark wood and decorated in prairie-style architecture. Floor-to-ceiling windows, sixty feet high, dramatically frame the Tetons in the distance. From these windows, one can scan the Willow Flats just outside of the lodge for elk, moose, and rare birds.

Brown oversized sofas and chairs fill the room where guests snuggle into the soft leather to read books or merely gaze quietly at the acres of meadow, wetlands, and mountains. Tall flames dance inside of the two massive fireplaces guarding each side of the upper lobby entrance. One of the hotel staff steps behind a steel mesh curtain to add wood and stoke the embers.

At our appointed reservation time, I roll Dad into the restaurant. A young maitre d' finds our reservation and guides us to the front of a line of waiting guests. Mom follows while I push Dad gently, careful not to bump his leg against a table, chair, or other diner. One of the four chairs at our table is removed, and I slide Dad up to his place setting.

We watch the scarlet sky fade until the mountains become only a silhouette in the distance. Living up to its name, the Mural Room features western paintings on its walls, and the white linen tablecloths give a dignified air to the restaurant.

As in many other national parks, individuals from all over the world staff the hotels and tourist concessions. Tonight, Tony from New Jersey is our waiter and hands us our menus.

"Remember," I say to Mom and Dad as they survey the entrees, "this meal is from us kids, so don't hold back."

Dad pulls his sweater tightly around him. His face glows red from the fever, and his foot remains swollen from sitting in the car too long. Riding across the parking lot completely destroyed any appetite he may have had.

He orders only a cup of soup and a side salad. I have the scallops. Mom, on the other side of the table, instructs Tony to bring her ten full ounces of free-range buffalo. My wide eyes meet Dad's incredulous expression.

These days, Mom and Dad usually pass up foods that are difficult to chew or bite. Age and lack of fluoride in their daily drinking water has caused their teeth to deteriorate. They no longer enjoy the pleasure of chomping into a crisp apple or raw carrot, and they certainly avoid steak dinners.

When our food is served, Mom finds the bison tender enough even for her. I think she ordered such a large amount hoping that Dad might be tempted to share some of it. He isn't interested. He didn't even finish his salad.

Tony returns at the end of the meal. "We have a statute in Wyoming that says you are required to order dessert."

Our waiter must not notice that Dad's eyes are closed. We break the law, and ask for the check.

Back in the lobby, Dad wants to see the gargantuan fireplaces up close. Maybe it reminds him of home, or maybe he wants to feel its powerful heat. Mom and I wander into the gift shops while he waits for us in front of the fire.

Nothing tempts us in the stores—nothing we can afford, anyway—and we head back to reclaim Dad.

"How much you wanna bet that he's back there talking to someone already?" Mom suggests, knowing Dad's usual disposition for socializing.

Strangers become Dad's friends within minutes. In his most recent hospital stay, he learned the life story of his roommate as well as his ailment and prognoses for discharge. He became a favorite of the nurses by asking about their children and how they chose their careers. Dad wanted one of his daughters to become a nurse. "You'll always have a job," he told us. None of us followed his advice.

Upon our return to the lobby, however, we find Dad asleep in his chair, quiet and alone. I wish Mom had been right. I wish he had struck up a conversation with a new friend about the weather conditions up on the mountains or the type of wood used in the giant fireplaces. We wake Dad gently and wheel him away from the warmth of the lodge.

The return trip to the cottage offers a new challenge. To the hotel's credit, outside lighting is minimal in order to maximize the best possible stargazing. Such illumination isn't ideal for our situation, however.

"Ouch, Rin," he says. "You need to slow down."

"I'm sorry, Dad. I just can't see the road or the bumps in it." Without light, I can't find a smoother path.

He reaches his limit.

"That's enough," he snaps. "Just let me do it myself."

I realize how much pain this road is causing him. Of course, in his mind, if I hadn't insisted on going out for dinner, we could have avoided this aggravation completely.

Dad tries to turn the wheels himself, but the road is too rough, and he isn't strong enough to push himself to the end of the row of cars, much less to our room. I reclaim my grip and move him forward as tenderly as I can.

Upon our return, Mom and Dad brush their teeth and put on their pajamas. Dad is tired but returns to his normal self now that he is safe inside the room. Mom, with her scarf wrapped around her head, tucks Dad into bed. Dad falls asleep quickly, but Mom stays awake to scan one of the books I have brought along

Frustrated that my efforts to provide my parents with a memorable evening have ended so miserably, I turn to knitting therapy. In the quiet of the room, I wrap the soft silky yarn around my fingers and attempt at least one beautiful thing tonight before turning off the light and falling asleep myself.

Friday

September 30

Thirteen years ago, I gave birth to my son, Eric. Mom had arrived several days earlier in order to stay with the girls whenever the contractions started. Good thing she was already there because Rob and I arrived at the hospital with only forty-five minutes before Eric was born.

Elisabeth was four and Clarissa was fifteen months. Learning to juggle three small children was difficult, and I was extremely grateful to have Mom at home with me. Without her, I would have been very lost, frustrated, and miserable. But for every minute she stayed with us, Dad was back on the farm feeling equally lost, frustrated, and miserable.

In their partnership, Dad is responsible for things outside of the house, fixing fence, care of the animals, planting and harvesting the crops, while Mom maintains order inside the house, patching jeans, house cleaning, and meal preparation. This arrangement suits both of them unless Mom isn't there to do her part. Until Eric was born, Mom always had cooked Dad's breakfast, a variety of eggs, pancakes, or hot cereal. To his credit, Dad learned how to cook Ralston 100% Wheat Hot Cereal in the microwave while Mom helped me with the kids. Dad spent the rest of the time bumming meals from his other two daughters, his sister, or friends who took pity upon him.

After a week, our freezer was full of food and all of our windows had been washed. Mom insisted that she had to return home, return to my father. I knew she couldn't stay with us forever, but I wasn't prepared for her to leave quite so soon.

"Rob will feel badly if you leave before he has a chance to say good-bye to you." She saw through my transparent attempts to persuade her to stay longer.

"No, I really need to get back."

With Eric balanced on my right forearm, I held Clarissa's tiny fingers in my left hand and used my right leg to prevent Elisabeth from running after Grandma's car. After Mom disappeared down the street, I herded the kids back into the house, three against one.

Rob has already wrapped Eric's presents and even made a special ice cream cake for him. The least I can do is wish him a happy birthday before he leaves for school.

"Hey, have a great day today. I mailed you a birthday card, but it won't arrive on time. Sorry."

"Oh, that's okay," Eric says. "I'm going to the football game tonight, so I won't be home much. I gotta go or I'll miss the bus."

Eric will have no difficulty celebrating his birthday without me, and actually, this relieves some of my motherly guilt. Besides, I'm needed here to help scrounge up some breakfast for Dad.

The morning is bright and crisp, ideal for an early stroll. I stop at the activity desk in the lodge to see where the trails are located.

"Some early walkers spotted four moose grazing in the Flats this morning." The gray-haired woman behind the counter directs me toward the low marsh covered with dense vegetation and tiny narrow streams connecting a series of ponds.

I hike out for a mile and a half but don't see any wildlife. I take a moment to look at the scene around me. The mountain air transforms my breath into fog. The sunrise lights the mountains peaks with a floating pink ribbon across the new snow. Songs of the morning birds compete for my attention, and the ground emits a distinct musty autumn scent. This must be the idyllic scene Dad imagined when he thought of visiting the Tetons, a perfect setting for him to experience and remember from this trip.

It's too late for me to run back to the duplex, wait for Dad to dress and hobble into the car. By that time the dawn will have evaporated into day. I should have planned better, more thoroughly, or adapted better to his needs so that he could witness this vista and breathe the fresh, biting air into his lungs. Now, the glow of the mountain and valley will pass without Dad ever being a part of it.

I've let my father down, especially knowing he will have no other opportunities to see this view. With this weight on my heart, I press my hands into my thighs just above my knees and feel tears well up behind my tightly closed eyes. I inhale sharply and then sigh. Voices echo down the path, and I force myself upright. The mountain peaks are impressive, but I'm no longer in the mood for what the scene has to offer.

Mom had trouble fitting Dad's swollen foot into his shoe this morning. Over a breakfast of bran muffins, Mom and I devise a plan that would allow Dad to elevate his leg while he rides in the car. If he could maneuver into the backseat, he could extend his right leg across the upholstery for better circulation. He will have to sit at an angle and miss the front-window view of the park, but it will help to reduce the swelling in his foot.

"What do you think, Charles?" Mom asks after describing and demonstrating the technique to him. "You want to try that?"

He doesn't even consider it. Without looking up at either of us, he says, "No, I'll just stay in the front."

Sighing, I slide into my seat and turn the key to start the engine. Dad struggles laboriously into the passenger side, and after he is adjusted, Mom climbs in behind him. We drive north to Yellowstone Park.

The interior of the car is eroding quickly. Yesterday, Dad and I passed our discarded coats, maps, park brochures, and a half-eaten bag of pretzels back to Mom for safekeeping. She was already sharing her seat with Dad's walker, her purse and mine, and the remains of our trash. She must have reached her limit because she makes a few changes.

Today the walker rides in the trunk rather than the backseat. She has another suggestion as well.

"Here, let's use these." She hands two brown sacks up to me in the front seat. "I found them in the room, and I think they are an ideal size for our trash."

Looking down at the sacks, I realize that Mom swiped the feminine hygiene bags from the room. I stifle my laugh, not sure if I am embarrassed or proud of her ingenuity. She's right, though. The bags fit smartly in the pocket of the car door, and she won't be overrun with our trash anymore. In my mother's world, practicality always trumps appearances.

The National Park Service strives to keep its land uncontaminated by human influence, a philosophy to which I usually subscribe. But I know of no other way to show Dad the park other than in an automobile on paved roads, two things usually at odds with the words *wilderness* and *habitat*. I search the maps for a road that at least will bring us closer to nature.

"We can't get out and hike, but I'm trying to find something that might take us into the backwoods a little ways. Maybe even spot us a bear."

"Sounds good," Mom says.

"You're the driver," Dad jabs.

The buffer between the Teton and Yellowstone parks is known as the John D. Rockefeller, Jr. Memorial Parkway, roughly eight square miles with no particular distinguishing characteristics. I wonder what political battle was behind its creation, but the map gives no hints.

Just past the Snake River, a sign points due west to Grassy Lake Road. The possibility of a worn and rugged trail, complete with wildlife and unfamiliar terrain, motivates me to turn left at the next intersection. We are exploring at last.

The paving ends at the Flagg Ranch Information Station, less than a quarter mile from the turnoff, and we proceed on gravel. A second road sign announces that the distance to Grassy Lake is ten miles, an ideal distance for a morning adventure.

In less than a mile, we cross a single-lane bridge, and the gravel turns to dirt. The road never widens again, and I feel we have discovered a vein in the Yellowstone gold mine.

At first we see six or seven campsites scattered next to the meandering stream, but eventually no signs of civilization remain. The way to Grassy Lake is filled with sharp corners, bumps, and uneven surfaces. My maximum speed is only ten miles per hour, which will make our exploration last a little longer than I expected. But we are here to see the sites, and we have the time.

"Look at that over in the field there." Dad spies a large, coffee-colored hide lumbering in the meadow to our left, a wonderful, whimsical-looking moose.

"Oh, there's another." Mom sees more moving behind the first one.

Around two more corners, an even larger mound of dusty brown rests on the grass by itself.

"Is that a buffalo just laying there, Charles?" The bison doesn't appear to be remotely affected by the sound or sight of our car.

Already we have seen more animals this morning than we did all day yesterday.

The narrow dirt road becomes more of a double cow path now, just barely wide enough to allow us to pass by two horse trailers.

"What are these people doing out here?" Mom wonders out loud. They probably ask the same thing about us.

In the next hour, we pass soft flowing meadows that give way to tall pines on each side of the road. Because our pace is so slow, I feel we have surely traveled twenty miles by now, but we still haven't seen any marks or other indicia of the lake.

"Welcome to the Caribou-Targhee National Forest," Dad reads from a sign that has been awkwardly and amateurishly attached to a tree.

"Mom, what does the map show?" We've been driving for over an hour, and we're still searching for the lake.

"Well, it looks like this road winds around and goes all the way back into Idaho."

As if timed perfectly to coincide with her words, we see another sign that reads, "Ashton, Idaho, 20 miles."

"I'm sorry, Dad," I say in frustration. "I keep thinking it's right around the corner or over the next hill, but I don't know where this thing is."

"It's elusive all right," he says.

Grassy Lake may be close, or maybe we passed by it without realizing it.

"Or maybe it doesn't really exist," Dad speculates. "I think some jokester park rangers put up those signs just to see how many tourists they can sucker down this trail."

"Maybe we should just turn around before we get all the way back to Idaho Falls," I propose.

My parents need no further convincing. After all, they're really more interested in the drive than the destination. When the road opens wide enough, I make a three-point turn and double back.

On the drive to this fabled lake, I deliberately drove slowly and patiently. Now I'm anxious to see the paved highway again, and I speed along at fifteen miles an hour. Occasionally I go as fast as twenty on the straight stretches, applying my brake and accelerator liberally at each pothole and groove in the road.

The car's lurching and pitching doesn't sit well with Dad.

"I need to pull over," he says when he can no longer suppress his nausea.

Ahead is a driveway that leads into a small open pasture nestled in the middle of the trees. I steer the car into the clearing, but before I turn off the engine, I lower the electric windows hoping that the blast of fresh air will still Dad's rollicking stomach.

The cool temperature is refreshing to me as well, and I step out of the car to give Dad time to recuperate. As if the chemotherapies weren't enough, now I've exacerbated Dad's already seasick condition. I'm tempted to walk into the woods, just a short distance, but remember that we hope to see a few bears on this trip. Instead, I wander next to a fallen tree, rotting in the middle of the grass.

After about ten minutes, Dad calls me back to the car.

"Okay, Rin. I'm better." I buckle my seat belt and back out onto the road.

"Here's some water." Mom hands him up a plastic bottle from the backseat to help with the nausea.

Dad won't tolerate the cool air for very long, but I move the thermostat lever to the blue side and the fan to high. And even though it means a longer ride, I don't let the speedometer go over twelve miles per hour.

Finally, the trees open up, and I recognize the meadow where we saw the bison.

"Hey, what happened to our moose?" I ask.

The campers are still here, and we drive past the nearly empty information station. When I see the main highway ahead of me, I feel comforted to be back within cell phone range.

Our next stop is the Grant Village store and gas pump. It sits at the edge of the West Thumb of Yellowstone Lake. Like the rest of the park, the place is nearly abandoned. A black sign with white letters announces that the village will close for the season in two days. When we step out of the car, we are nearly blown away by the biting wind.

"I'm gonna go in here," Dad says as he walks slowly to the paint-bare bathrooms. Mom and I search for sustenance from the dwindling pantry in the shop.

"What are you hungry for, Mom?" Most of the remaining food consists of chips or other types of junk food, not generally appealing to either of my parents.

"How about these sandwiches here?" She points to a pair of end-of-season tuna fish sandwiches abandoned in the refrigerator section. Our choice is limited so I acquiesce. I also buy a diet Mt. Dew for myself, knowing I'll need extra help to stay awake this afternoon in the hot car.

Across the road from the store, an asphalt parking lot serves as our picnic area. Five or six steam holes spit geothermal vapor from below the pavement. The lot is on the lakeshore and provides us with entertainment as we eat our dull lunch.

"Look how that wind makes those waves out there, Ma."

The sharp gusts in the lake create a surge of white caps. We continue to feel the wind rocking the car.

I look closely at my lunch, gray tuna paste with bits of celery spackled on white bread. The clouds around us mirror the color of our sandwich spread. We eat in silence, matching the chill and cheerlessness of the scenery before us.

After lunch, we drive to Old Faithful, one of the most famous attractions at Yellowstone. A swath of blue sky emerges over us although the temperature and wind outside the car are still sharp and blasting.

"I don't want to get out." Dad resists the idea of leaving the car merely to see a waterspout, but he doesn't want to miss it entirely.

"See if you can get close," he instructs.

I find an open parking space fairly close to the boardwalk entry and notice that other tourists wait in their cars as well. Without a doubt, something is lost when watching nature from inside a car instead of close up where one can actually feel the mist from the spout.

"Mom, you want to walk around and get a closer look?" Really, I'm the one who wants to leave the car, but she relents.

The same wintry wind from the lake blows through us as we stroll along the boardwalk above geysers and steaming activity. The round trip takes only fifteen minutes to complete, but the entire way we are stalked by a woman speaking abnormally loud on her cell phone.

The end of the loop stops in front of the Old Faithful Inn, a giant ski lodge with dark interior.

"Let's get some ice cream for your father," Mom suggests. It's not my place to argue.

Dad accepts his chocolate cone willingly, and even though the air outside is cold, the atmosphere inside of the car seems a bit warmer. We eat our ice cream while small numbers of tourists walk to and from the geyser.

When I lean forward to start the engine, ready to find our accommodations for the night, I remember that the Old Faithful parking lot is one of the best places in the country to play the license plate game.

"Hey! We can find some more states here." The potential for finding out-of-state plates buoys me, and my parents are captives as I troll the aisles of cars.

"New Jersey. Do we have New Jersey?" I call back to Mom. Certainly we don't have the same buffet of license plates to choose from as we would in the summer. Still, we find a few new ones.

"There's Kentucky, West Virginia, and Tennessee. Oh, we already have Tennessee. Mom, are you getting these?"

"Okay," she confirms.

"Montana, Utah," I continue. "But we already have Utah, don't we?"

"I can't find a pen," she lies. I look back to see a pen rolling around on her yellow legal pad as she licks her ice cream and gazes out the window.

"Why are we doing this?" Dad asks, not with sarcasm but pure curiosity.

"It's fun." I can't believe I have to explain this to him.

Keeping one eye on the license plates that pass us, I drive back to another section of the park where the Lake Yellowstone Hotel and Cabins await us. Dad once read a magazine article that touted the beauty and thrill of a boat ride on the choppy cold waters of Lake Yellowstone. Boating season ended in mid-September, and the next best thing I could arrange was lodging for us next to its shores.

The origins of this building date back to the late 1800s, but renovations in the 1920s were responsible for its current reputation of stately and august lodgings. The bright yellow three-story hotel faces Yellowstone Lake, and a massive pine tree forest surrounds the rest of the compound. Four white pillars, as tall as the hotel itself, stand at attention as guests circle past the flagpole.

Mom and I have to go inside the giant hotel for our cabin assignments. Two steps into the front entry demonstrate that the interior is as impressive as the outside. The bright interior and wicker chairs invite guests to recline in them. The elegant dining room requires reservations, which I won't bother making. Instead we proceed directly to the desk.

Jodi from Washington, as identified by her Xanterra Resorts nametag, greets us.

"Hi. I didn't request it when I made reservations, but we need a cabin that has no steps, or at least only one or two small steps." I explain Dad's requirements.

"Oh, let me look for something." Jodi searches for a book that she claims contains details of each cabin, including the precise number of steps to each door. After about sixty seconds, she gives up.

"No, sorry. Can't find it. But you know, these cabins hardly have any steps at all. It shouldn't be a problem."

Jodi tears off a map from a legal-sized pad of paper and with her pen draws the route over the village roads, past the general village store, and ending at Frontier Cabin 544.

"If that doesn't work, just come back here, and we'll find another."

As we drive to our assigned place, we notice that the duplexes, like the hotel, are also painted yellow, although a much more subtle shade than what is used on the hotel's exterior. I stop in front of 544. Three steps, three very thin steps, lead up to the white door of our assigned cabin.

"Well, this won't work at all," Mom declares without even leaving the car. "What was that girl thinking?"

I turn the car around. On the return trip to the desk, Mom jots down the numbers of the cabins with ramps rather than stairs. She intends to mention these in her report to Jodi.

Realizing that the young clerk has no idea about our failed Grassy Lake excursion today or the lousy lunch I shared with my parents, I try to maintain my cool as I explain again why narrow, steep steps, even though only three, are a significant challenge to my father.

"He can't put any weight on his right foot," I say as I push the key back across the front desk. "We noticed there were some cabins without any steps. Are any of those available?"

Kris from Germany is also at the desk and overhears our conversation.

"No," says Kris firmly but with concern. "The handicapped cabins are all reserved."

Despite the relatively few of us touring the park, we must have hit the peak season for visitors in wheelchairs. She leans under the long, wooden bench, shuffles a flurry of papers, and stands up with a sort of cabin bible in her hands, the book Jodi couldn't find earlier.

"This might work for you, though. It has only one step."

Kris rips off another map and marks the route to the newly assigned cabin. Mom and I go back to the car, and she navigates me to Number 559.

"How about this, Dad?" All Dad wants is to leave the car and prop up his foot.

"It's fine," he grumbles, and he uses the last of his energy to maneuver out of the car and hobble inside. As soon as he crosses the threshold, he gives orders to increase the heat and bring him more blankets. Then he falls on his back onto the bed.

The cabin is spare. No television, radio, or telephone interrupts the natural sounds here in the wilderness. Sensible brown carpet covers the floor. Western-design bedspreads cover each of the double beds. In addition to a writing desk and chair in the room, a luggage table sits at the foot of one of the beds. Two paintings of Yellowstone's natural beauty are the only decorative items in the room.

Instructions hanging on the bathroom door encourage us to save energy by reusing our towels and linens. A step-in shower is stocked with a single bar of soap and a small container of shampoo.

Lake stones, the size of bread and butter plates, are scattered in the yard outside the cabin. Dad's ankle has not returned to normal size since we left Iowa. It occurs to me that one of these rocks could serve as a type of natural ice pack for his foot. I retrieve one of the stones from outside of the door.

"Dad, what if we wrap a towel around one of these and use it to get that swelling down a bit?"

He submits to the compress for less than two minutes. Either too cold or too goofy, Dad pushes the icy stone away from his swollen ankle before it has a chance to make any difference.

"That's enough of that," he says.

Dad's unwillingness to accept my help heightens my growing desire for time alone. I'm certain Mom and Dad also long for their privacy.

"I'm going to walk around the camp a little bit, if that's okay with you guys."

"Yeah," Dad highly encourages. "Go, go."

The cabins are close to the lake, making it easy to explore the trail next to the shore. Sharp, cold wind from the water blows through me, but I welcome its clean smell and vibrant touch, especially after the constant dry heat of the car.

I'd really like to talk to Rob right now, but no signal bars pop up on my cell phone when I try to use it. Instead, I'm forced to use the pay phone adjacent to the village store. Listening first for the dial tone, I punch in the numbers of my plastic pre-paid phone card.

Busy signal.

I walk around a little more before trying Rob again. This time Eric answers.

"Dad went to pick up Elisabeth and Clare from school. I had a pretty good birthday. Dad said it was okay if I go to the football game tonight."

"Have fun," I say without much enthusiasm. "I'll call back in about ten minutes because I really want to talk to Dad."

While I wait for Rob, I browse the general store, looking for selections that are soft and easy to chew. I select three bananas.

With my purchase swinging in the sack attached to my arm, I try Rob one more time.

Another busy signal. For whatever reason, not being able to talk to Rob right now is sending me over the edge of what has been a culmination of a very gray day, both literally and figuratively.

Dad sleeps most of the time. The air inside is hot and dry and bitingly cold outside. We must hold the record for having seen the least number of wildlife of any visitor to Yellowstone. The park scenery is beautiful and inspiring but two dimensional from the car.

Now, I can't even complain to Rob about any of it. I sigh deeply and walk my bananas back to the cabin.

I find Dad freshly showered. With Mom's help, he has had his first thorough bathing experience since we left home. The past two nights, our bathrooms had full-sized tubs, a feature highly valued by many travelers but not by Dad. A tall-sided tub is useless to him on account of his inability to lift his leg high enough to clear the edge. Fortunately for us, the shower in this bare cabin has only a very low rim over which Dad can step easily.

Dad wears a clean white T-shirt and boxer shorts. Rejuvenated, he sits in a chair rather than lay on the bed.

"Am I there yet?" he asks Mom backing up to the leather upholstered chair.

"Almost. Can you feel that against your leg? Is it too far down?"

Dad groans as he sits, his traditional call for attention. He rests his right foot on the luggage table at the end of his bed.

"That's better," he says. Then he releases a belch. "That was legitimate, too. I'm not apologizing for that one."

I ignore him.

"Whadya bring from the store, Rin?"

"Well, we haven't had much fruit, so I brought some bananas."

Dad curls his lip at me and snarls in disgust. Mom has a more diplomatic, but equally negative response.

"You don't like bananas? Either one of you?"

"Not particularly. But we'll eat them," Dad assures me.

With limited entertainment options for the evening, I unpack the laptop computer from my suitcase.

"So that's why your bag is so heavy," Mom says as if I had been hiding it. "What are you working on?"

In planning this trip, I knew the three of us would be spending many long hours together in the car. I imagined how we might fill the time with Mom and Dad recounting hundreds of their life stories. I brought along my computer to write and save these anecdotes, possibly sharing them later with my siblings or my own children.

The reality of this trip demonstrates the naïveté and impracticality of my idea. None of our car conversations could remotely be considered a life reflection. Now, when presented with an ideal opportunity to ask probing and meaningful questions, the moment seems contrived. If I tell my parents I plan to transcribe whatever they say, they'll be self-conscious and veiled.

I lie instead.

"I thought I might do a little office work while I'm here." I cross my legs on the bed with my iBook in front of me.

"Fine," Dad says. "I'm going to sit here and eat a candy bar. You want one, Rin?"

"No, thanks." I refuse to acknowledge that this generic-brand breakfast food is any sort of a candy bar. I took a bite of one yesterday and gagged on its nasty flavor. Dad's taste buds must be worse off than I thought if he is able to eat them.

"Do you want this lotion now?" Mom asks Dad before she rubs hand lotion very tenderly on Dad's swollen foot and lower leg.

After the initial cancer was removed from his right shin, Dad's wound was red and gory. The surgery left a gaping hole in his leg roughly the size and shape of a rugby ball. Several follow-up surgeries extracted any remaining tissue.

Now his leg appears less severe, but the indentation remains a deep purple-red, burnt from the radiation treatments. Mom applies the lotion on this part of his leg as well.

In our toasty cabin by Lake Yellowstone, Dad begins to sing a familiar and melodic hymn until he forgets the second line.

"What's the words to that, Ma?"

Mom sings him the entire verse. He begins the song again but as before, loses the words after the first line. He resorts to humming instead.

The shower has revived Dad mentally as well as physically. His familiar, playful personality returns. He demonstrates how he can sing a bass note while eating the bad breakfast bar at the same time.

"You inherited a lot of talent, Rin."

The tension that built inside of me throughout the day eases away with every wrong note Dad performs.

"I don't know if I want any more of that," he says after eating half of his so-called candy bar.

Mom assures him he doesn't have to eat anything he doesn't want, and my confidence in his sense of taste returns.

After Mom rubs the cream around his ankle and foot, but before she can twist the lid tightly on the jar, Dad makes another request.

"I'm parched. I need some water."

Dutifully, Mom stands up and removes the plastic wrap sealed around one of the cups in the cabin, filling it with water from the bathroom.

Mom also has lotion for Dad's face.

"I don't want that stuff," he resists. "When I kiss you on the lips tonight, do you want that junk rubbing off?"

This is all for my benefit.

"I don't mind," Mom says. Then she changes the subject. "Do you want to try an ice pack tonight?"

I look up from my keyboard.

"Yeah, maybe I should," He says with resignation.

I set my computer aside, grab the ice bucket, and head for the ice machine in the main lodge. When I return, Mom pours the cubes into a bag she saved from one of Dad's recent hospital stays. When it can hold no more, she places the cold compress next to Dad's ankle.

Dad reads from a pamphlet Mom and I picked up when we were inside the lodge. It summarizes the history of the park and its early explorers.

"I wonder what ol' John Coulter was thinking about when he was sitting here, taking notes on all this geothermal activity."

Mom doesn't know about John, but she had a good guess about Mrs. Coulter.

"His wife was probably saying, 'You stupid old man. Why don't you come home and take care of your family?'"

Dad releases another belch, as loud as a foghorn. I stare at him. He grins.

At six o'clock, Dad lifts himself from the chair and moves to the side of the bed. Like a contortionist, he flops backward with enough force to bring his legs up to the bed and wrangles under the covers until he finds a comfortable position. His eyes are closed, but he stays awake and alert. He doesn't want to miss out on any conversation.

Mom sits in the chair beneath the window, staring forward into the darkening room. We have yet to switch on the lights, preferring instead to sit in the shadows of the fading day. I adjust my position on the bed.

Now seems an appropriate, even natural time to probe some personal stories. Mom and Dad hear me type their words, but the twilight conceals our faces enough to ask and answer the questions.

We begin with their respective childhoods, how they met, about neighbors, friends, and extended family. I enjoy hearing these familiar tales again, but I listen closely for new details or corrections to my own versions of history.

Then I risk a little more.

"What are your worst fears?"

"It's not death," Dad answers quickly. After a little longer, he continues. "It's probably going to a nursing home."

Mom agrees. "No privacy, no control over your life. It's degrading. It's a death sentence. A prison of a sort. You're told when to get up, and you don't know from one day to the next who's going to take care of you. I suppose if I have to, I have to. It's the lack of privacy that would bother me more than anything."

My maternal grandmother was a fiercely independent woman, but like many whose bodies betray them with age, she reached a stage where she could no longer clean, cook, or care for herself in a safe way. Assisted living wasn't enough support, but a full-time care facility would virtually eliminate the few activities Grandma could still enjoy. Instead, she moved in with Mom and Dad.

Grandma passed the time observing the outside world through the large bay window in my parent's living room. Her eyesight was sharp enough to identify different birds and watch critters play in the yard.

"Zola," she would call, or sometimes she used a small bell to capture her daughter's attention. The dutiful daughter stopped her own work to attend to Grandma.

"What do you need, Mother?"

"Look at how fast those squirrels run up that cottonwood tree. And there are two over that hill chasing each other around the grain bin."

For the next four and a half years, Grandma's meals were served to her on a tray. She slept in the room next to that of my parents. As much as everyone loved everyone else, the already small house felt even smaller with Grandma there. I imagine the strain at home was similar to my own experience this week, only worse for my parents because at least I have a date certain to return home whereas no end date was ever proposed for their arrangement.

Eventually, Mom wore out. She repeatedly reported her shortness of breath to her doctor until he could no longer ignore her symptoms. A treadmill test and angiogram revealed the need for immediate heart bypass surgery.

The operation went as planned, but her chest still hurt when she was in recovery. Another test was done to determine whether a second surgery would be necessary. None of us were prepared for Mom's first surgery, much less a second one.

Adjacent to the waiting room was a private family conference room. With his children beside him, Dad prayed earnestly for Mom's recovery. I had seen Dad pray many times before, but I had never understood the depth of his love for Mom until that moment. His quiet tears and shaking hands revealed just how frightened he was for her life.

Fortunately, Mom didn't need a second surgery, but she was in no shape to care for Grandma. Neither were any of her siblings. Grandma readily agreed to move into a nursing home because she expected to return when Mom was feeling better. Although Mom did recover, she was never able to care for her mother in the same way again. Grandma never returned to the farm.

The Yellowstone cabin is completely dark now except for the light from my computer screen.

"Do you believe in life after death?" The question is almost routine when asked in the context of a religious discussion, but the question portends beyond the philosophical given Dad's present circumstance.

"I believe there is a type of existence after we die," Mom says. "I don't know what, and I'm not ready to figure it all out yet."

Dad is more specific, more certain.

"I believe the soul goes some place other than here. It won't be caught up in pain and con-founded sickness and darkness. I think there will be a great reunion. I hope. I'm looking forward to that. I haven't been awake one night worryin' about what happens later. The old body will rot down there on the hill, and the soul will be long gone. I got a lot of people to see."

My own doubts regarding an afterlife still linger, but tonight I find great comfort knowing that Mom and Dad have no reservations or fear of this particular unknown.

Saturday

October 1

"Want to walk with me this morning, Mom?"

"Yeah, I think I will." She reaches for her jacket to wear over her faded blue sweatshirt. The air from the lake is still cold but not nearly so windy. We take time to admire the sun as it gleams from behind the eastern hills.

"How are things going for you at work, Rin?" Mom asks me as we walk along the shoreline.

Without meaning to, I unleash concerns about issues at work. Then I proceed to unload all the worries I have for my children. Mom listens to my ramblings without offering patronizing advice or making judgments. Perhaps she appreciates the distraction from the weights of her own life.

My parents and I have always confined our conversations to practical nouns and verbs, rarely expressing our genuine appreciation for one another. Our lifetimes of experience have created a confidence in our relationship that doesn't require constant verbal reassurance. At least, that's my theory.

At sixteen, I wasn't so sure. Bored with high school, I applied to be an exchange student in New Zealand for a year. Both parents were supportive, but Dad's particular encouragement surprised me, especially given the cost of the program.

At Omaha's Epply Airport, the same airport we used at the beginning of this week's journey, my parents gave me giant hugs and bestowed practical advice on me just before I boarded the plane. Mom and Dad avoided any tears, believing that such emotion would only make it more difficult for me to leave.

On the other hand, I was about to take my very first airplane ride and it happened to be a 12,000-mile flight. I was also going to be living with total strangers and wouldn't see or even be in telephone contact with my family for a whole year. I was in need of a little reassurance.

But because my parents didn't cry, I didn't cry either. I mirrored their stoicism until I had stowed my luggage and fastened my seat belt. Through the scratched, oval window in the airplane, I searched the terminal for their faces, hoping to see a hint of sadness about my departure and long absence. I tried to stifle my sobs from the businessman in the seat next to me, but he could sense something very painful had just occurred.

Years later, Rhonda and I were reminiscing about our childhood when she randomly recalled her memory of that day. She described a very different scene than what I remembered. She said Mom and Dad were heartbroken, even scared. They even allowed a few tears to roll down their faces after I disappeared into the airplane.

My year in New Zealand was fantastic. It was my host mother who taught me to knit. My parents and Kiwi family ultimately became very close friends. But at a time when all of us needed support and encouragement, I wish one of us had been open about our feelings.

Since Dad's diagnosis, I feel the three of us are more comfortable about openly expressing our emotions. Instead of ending our weekly phone conversation with a casual sign off, it's slower and more deliberate. "I love you" now means more than just goodbye.

Each night around one or two, Dad has to use the bathroom. He manages this independently, which is good for all of us. He sits up and swings his legs onto the floor. Then he scoots as close to the edge of the bed as he can and reaches for his walker. Although he can reach the bathroom and return without help, he readily shares his groans and panting with his roommates. Mom and I both wake up and take our turn in the bathroom or to get a drink of water, and all three of us exchange witty remarks before drifting back to sleep.

Last night was no exception, but Dad was especially restless. Mom hunted for the thermometer she had packed. His temperature read 101. I used this as an excuse to turn down the heat, and Mom administered more medication. After minor adjustments to his pillow and blankets, we eventually all nodded back to sleep.

"How are you feeling this morning, Dad?" I say when Mom and I return from our walk.

"Good, good. The thermometer reads 99."

He looks and sounds better. Even though his foot is still swollen, it's no larger than it was last night. After our breakfast in the room—mine includes a banana—we pack up Dad and the luggage for today's drive north on the eastern loop road in search of Canyon Falls.

Through the trees, we catch glimpses of the water falling into the Yellowstone River against the bright blue sky. In order to have a proper view of its power, we stop at an overlook below the road.

"Why don't you and Rin go out to the edge there, Ma, and look at it." Dad is content to stay in the car.

Mom and I climb out but only gaze at the waterfall for less than a minute. The wind is cold, plus we don't enjoy the sight knowing Dad can't share it with us.

After the falls, we drive north through Dunraven Pass, a heavily forested part of the park. Unless we drive on top of a ridge, we can't see any further than the three rows of trees on either side of us.

"You can see where the fire has come through here, can't you?" Mom observes. "It certainly has left a mark."

I look out the passenger window to see hundreds of parkland acres scarred from the flames. Lone pine trees are scattered on the hillside, black and charred with no sign of new needles or fresh growth of any kind. The hot blaze of the fire consumed this formerly green and lush earth right down to its skeletal form.

The park rangers and brochures say that this is a healing process, that the forest needs the fire in order to have long-term health. I look at the landscape outside Dad's window, just past his head bald from chemotherapy, and try to understand how such a devastatingly painful process can ever be beneficial to a life cycle again.

The green Buick takes us past the tallest mountain in Yellowstone, Mt. Washburn. The guidebook describes a number of trails to the top.

"I wouldn't mind doing one of those climbs," I say as we drive by another sign with a stick-figure hiker painted on it.

"Yeah, that'd be cool," Dad agrees. "What I'd really like to do, though, is take a pumpkin up there on top, and then let 'er go and see how far it would roll. That's a true test of a mountain."

Fun for Dad, perhaps, but I doubt that drivers on the highway below would find much humor in it.

Dad and I continue our war over the thermostat. I turn down the heat when I see his eyes are closed. He wakes up from the chill and flips it back to the red side. Extraordinarily warm air, coupled with his pain medication and the rocking of the car, lull Dad to sleep again.

A particularly exquisite swath of yellow, green, orange, purple, and brown grows on a ridge in front of us. When I turn my head back to make sure Mom sees it, she too, is sleeping. Her hands clutch the National Park Service brochure, and her glasses are poised at the edge of her nose.

Dad sleeps because he is sick. Mom sleeps from sheer exhaustion. She needs a rest, not only for the past year and a half devoted to caring for Dad, but for the past fifty years of work as well.

While other people vacationed, Mom began her summers in April planting potatoes and onions. Tender annuals were planted in May. Around Memorial Day weekend, the sweet and juicy strawberries stained our hands red as we picked, stemmed, and froze quarts of the red fruit for winter consumption. Dad insisted on fresh, biscuit-style shortcake for his strawberries, and every day during the season, Mom stirred up the batter, eventually turning the task over to Rhonda.

Next, Mom "did" the chickens. She purchased around one hundred fluffy yellow chicks in early spring and kept them fed, watered, and warm in the coop. By June, the birds were at optimal weight and tenderness. She betrayed them with her machete knife held together with duct tape before dressing them out completely.

The first cutting of hay followed the poultry massacre. Dad hired teenaged neighbor boys for the heavy lifting, but Mom used the same amount of time and energy to make the midday meal. No matter the temperature of the Iowa summer day, her menu included fresh chicken fried in the black cast-iron skillet, mashed potatoes, homemade rolls, and apple pie.

We hoed the weeds from the soybean fields before the Fourth of July. By the end of the month, bushels of sweet corn were handpicked, shucked, and cooked before landing in the deep freeze. August found Mom in a very hot kitchen without air conditioning as she canned and froze gallons of beans, zucchini, tomatoes, apples, and any other fruit or vegetable that was ripe and overproducing.

Mom boasted to anyone who dined with us in September that every item on the table was grown on our farm, from poultry to peaches, beef to beans, and pork to pickles.

She did all of this on top of her routine cooking, laundry, housekeeping, shopping, and child rearing. With an occasional complaint but mostly accepting the reality of her world, Mom deserved her rest.

At the next bump, both Mom and Dad are awake again. Mom straightens the map and pushes her glasses closer to her eyes. Ahead of us is an expansive grazing meadow. A lone bison crosses the road in front of us to reach the spot.

"Watch for more," Mom says, "because they're never alone. At least that's what it says in this book." She holds up a guidebook in the air as her proof. She's right. After we drive around the next bend, an entire herd heads in our direction. We stop at a convenient pull out to watch the parade.

This is the season for these magnificent creatures to shed their brown tattered and shaggy hides. Their eyes are dark, perhaps even black, and steam blows from their nostrils. Most of the buffalo we see are cows and calves, but an occasional bull mixes in the herd as well.

"They're just takin' their time, aren't they," Mom says of the beasts. Each statue-sized animal has a different pace, and during the time we watch them, two or three detour to find a short cut to the pasture we passed earlier.

"There must be at least a hundred of them," I observe. It's by far the best display of wildlife we have had yet. After waiting twenty minutes, we return to the road and watch the entire valley open up with a wide array of animals and vegetation. Moose graze in the far plains, and even more bison roam in the distance.

"Now, Dad," Mom only calls him this when any of us children are in the room, "this brochure says that where we are is 'prime grizzly country,' so you need to keep a lookout."

Dad's dream of spotting a bear is reignited. As he searches for one, he spies a gangly elk drinking from one of the park's shallow creeks.

"I would love to have my gun with me, be able to get close to that big, majestic animal over there. Have him give himself up to the food chain."

"The food chain?" I cry incredulously. "You think he wants to be a sacrifice? If he's so majestic, why is it such a thrill to kill the animal?"

"Well," he says, "you know."

"What? Know what?"

Dad shrugs.

My voice sounds harsher than I had intended. My father and I obviously have divergent views regarding the glory of entering the food chain. I meant only to gently spar for welcome conversation, but he backed down sooner than expected. Now I regret that I said anything.

Growing up, we never challenged our father. Mom usually disciplined us and often softened Dad enough to excuse us from chores in order to arrive at a school event on time. She also persuaded him to ease up nonessential tasks on days when the temperatures soared over a hundred degrees or below zero. At least one time, though, they completely reversed their traditional roles.

After my first year of college, I returned home for the summer, generously bestowing my newly acquired wisdom and knowledge on my parents. The combination of having a serious boyfriend but not having transportation to see him further complicated life at home.

After a few weeks, I was determined to travel by bus to see my beau who lived in another town. I didn't bother to consult Mom before making my plans because, true to freshman form, I naturally assumed she would drive me whenever and wherever I wanted to go. It never occurred to me, nor did I care, that my forty-six-year-old mother might also have a life.

Mom refused my request, not because she was tired of being my chauffer or doormat, but because she actually had other appointments for the day. What started as a request for a ride rapidly deteriorated into a shouting match that included the words "selfish," "thoughtless," and "just leave." This was one time Mom and I had no difficulty expressing our feelings for each other.

Dad heard us screaming at each other from in the barn. He hurried into the house to mediate what was left of the situation. After hearing the story from Mom, Dad found me in my basement room.

"She hates me," I bawled.

"No, she doesn't hate you. You know that." He tried to reason with me.

At that moment, my mother probably did hate me. I would have hated me, too. My father's tender words, unusual as they were, calmed me until my sobs turned to hiccups and the red splotches on my checks began to disappear.

I don't remember whether I ever boarded the bus, but I do know that if Dad hadn't intervened that afternoon, I would have married that boyfriend even sooner than I did.

"Hey, Dad. I think one of those brown blobs over by those trees must be a bear," I say in an attempt to apologize for the food chain remark. Until we reach our next stop, we pretend that every vague boulder or distant rock is a brown, black, or even a grizzly bear. Unfortunately, the real thing continues to evade us.

We break from the drive at Tower-Roosevelt Station, stretching our limbs and using the bathroom. After three days, we have our routine learned, each of us with our respective roles. I turn off the ignition and press the trunk release button by my left leg. While I retrieve the walker, Mom disengages herself from behind Dad's seat and opens his car door. I unfold and hand her the walker as she carefully guides Dad's right foot out of the car.

With a grimace painted on his face, Dad presses his left leg against the side panel of the car and pushes himself deep into his seat. He fits his left foot under his right and lifts it up and over the bottom portion of the doorframe. Adjusting again to turn his entire body facing out, he winces and pulls his weight toward the door.

His left hand grips the top of the open car door while the other tightly grasps his walker. Slowly, he transfers his weight onto his left leg. After fine-tuning his balance as well as his hat, he shuffles in the direction of the bathroom. Mom shuts the door and follows him.

The wind at this station nearly knocks Dad off of his feet. The bridge to Tower Falls is temporarily washed out, but I catch a fairly decent view of the falls half a mile up an asphalt path. In the time it takes me to cover the distance to the lookout, enjoy the scene, and walk back, Dad has finally returned to the car.

We have less than twenty miles to our final destination for the day, Mammoth Hot Springs. More and more elk appear the closer we move towards the town. Hundreds of them graze on the prairie and lumber along the side of the road. By the time we reach the village itself, we see lawns and open areas full of these comical creatures dozing and plodding in the midst of the old historic town. A strategically placed park ranger dressed in her uniform greens and a wide-brim hat keeps peace between tourist and beast.

I look at my watch. It's not even noon.

"I think we're too early to check in at the lodge," I advise. "You want to drive around a bit?"

"Yeah," says Dad. "I don't want to be gettin' in and out of this contraption any more than I have to."

Mammoth Hot Springs is an old cavalry post converted into Yellowstone Park Headquarters. Two-story sandstone buildings with red-shingled roofs and brick fireplaces line the single street of the tiny town. A few other buildings sit back a block to the east and provide lodging for most of the concession workers. Directly west of the main street is a large open field with white-bearded sagebrush and, of course, more elk. At the northernmost edge, we find a restaurant and our evening accommodations.

Pine trees cover the hills that surround and protect the tiny village from Yellowstone's winters. Steam from hundreds of geothermal pools rises from the ground and creates an oasis of warmth for the animals during the harshest weather.

"It looks like we can drive around some of those geysers just up the hill here," Mom says.

At the one stop sign in town, I turn left and climb the steep hill toward Mammoth's main attraction, the Lower Terrace. Here, boardwalks weave in and out of the boiling mud, smoldering holes, and strong smells of sulfur, allowing tourists to experience these wonders close up.

I pull into the parking lot where we tower over the town nestled deep in its mountain valley. We quickly realize that the Lower Terrace only offers a walking tour, one that Dad could not manage.

"There's another road further on," Mom says. "It looks like we can drive right next to some of these things."

We return to the main road for a quarter of a mile until we see the sign to the Upper Terrace. Full of loops and switchbacks, the one-way lane winds next to sites known as Orange Mound Spring and Angel Terrace. The landscape is literally scorched as the geothermal temperatures roast the roots of any deep vegetation. The pools of mineral deposits dazzle us in colors of precious gems—emeralds, amber, rubies, and sapphires. While no substitute for what could be seen or smelled had we walked next to them, the drive provides at least a glimpse of this unusual terrain.

As interesting as this was, we are only twenty minutes later than we were before.

"We can't get into our cabin yet, so do you want to try to get some lunch?" I ask hopefully.

Two dining options are available to us, both located in the same building and operated by the same concessionaire. One is a formal restaurant, and the other is a delicatessen. We choose the deli.

Mom and Dad order only sandwiches but help themselves to my French fries.

"Do you think Rod figured out that we turned off the water to the bathroom?" Mom wonders aloud. I'm curious to know what sent her mind to thinking of their water pipes.

My brother is the oldest of the four children. Even though he and his wife, Kathi, live two hours northeast of Mom and Dad in Nebraska, Rod makes frequent trips to the farm where he helps to mend fences, stack wood within easy reach of the back door, or do whatever else is needed. This weekend, he will check on the house to ensure that no unwelcome intruder, human or animal, has invaded the place.

"He'll figure it out," Dad answers. "And he'll have to light a fire if he wants to stay warm, too." Dad must be cold again.

We've long since finished our lunches, but we remain at the counter that runs along the large south window of the deli. From here we observe the traffic patterns of Mammoth Hot Springs, note that the average age of the tourist in Yellowstone in October is over sixty years old, and squint to identify the state of each license plate that drives past us.

Then, as if to break the monotony, an official park vehicle flashes its lights as it speeds past the restaurant. We don't even have to move to see the nature of the emergency. We simply cast our eyes up the road where a massive buffalo has plopped himself down on the centerline of the main artery through town. No vehicle can drive around him, and none of the pedestrians dare approach him. We enjoy the moment and even speculate how the rangers will coax the beast from his nap.

I leave Mom and Dad to watch the excitement while I check on the availability of accommodations in the main lobby.

"I need a room without steps," I explain at the hotel counter for the third night in a row.

Linda, from Oregon, understands my request and begins her search for available rooms.

"I'm sorry. I'm not seeing anything without any steps at all." I'm disheartened again.

"I do have one duplex that only has two steps. You can try that, and if it doesn't work, come back and we'll find something else."

I have no alternative, so I accept the keys to Number B18.

The bison has left, and with nothing left to entertain them, Mom and Dad are now ready to help me find our cabin.

The lodgings at Mammoth Hot Springs are duplex bungalows painted gray to blend into the hills to the north and east. The front porch extends along the entire length of the duplex with green plastic chairs set out to encourage visitors to enjoy the scenery. Woodcuts of the park animals decorate each side of the porch.

Rather than straight lines, groups of six bungalows are placed in wagon-train style, circling around a common lawn for outdoor recreation. The arrangement is conducive for visiting with neighbors, but because parking is behind each cabin, I can't park close to the door. Dad will have to carefully navigate twenty-five feet of uneven ground until he reaches the cabin.

I evaluate the two steps, three including the porch, that lead to the room inside. Actually, if Dad turns his walker sideways, he can exploit it as a second railing to steady himself. This can work, I think to myself.

Rather than using the assigned parking space, I position the car as close to the front of the bungalow as I can, trying to eliminate extra steps for Dad. He wills himself out of the car, lifting the weight of his torso with his hands firmly mounted on the walker. He has difficulty balancing on the uneven grass, but he finally reaches the bottom step.

With one hand on the porch banister and one hand on his walker, he leverages as much weight as possible on his hands and lifts his good left leg onto the first step. The right leg swings to catch up. He repeats this two more times until he reaches the gray boards of the porch floor.

"Hmmm," he exhales loudly.

Once he is safely inside the cabin, he gives the familiar orders to increase the heat before promptly falling under the blankets Mom has already found for him. It's not yet midafternoon, but Dad has no intention of leaving this room the rest of the day.

This bungalow appears newer than the cabin where we stayed last night, but the décor is mostly the same. Tonight, the carpet is blue instead of brown, and a lamp sits on the simple square table between the double beds. Again, only two Yellowstone paintings adorn the otherwise stark, ivory walls.

While Dad sleeps, Mom and I explore the tourist village, starting with the Albright Visitor Center and Museum. The printed information states that the building was built in the late 1800s to protect the park from vandalism and theft. We wander upstairs to admire more Yellowstone landscapes painted in watercolor. When we return to the main floor, we discover we're just in time to watch a movie of the history and legacy of the park. About five minutes into the film, I hear Mom breathing slowly and deliberately. No one else is in the theatre, and I wouldn't mind a nap myself.

After our rest, Mom and I visit the town's gift shop and store. I purchase token items for each of the kids, and Mom finds a stuffed moose for my nephew, Keasen. She also buys individual cereal boxes for Dad's breakfast, giving him something in his stomach when he takes his morning medicine.

Breakfast reminds me of lunch.

"Hey, I saw at the restaurant that they make up box lunches. Instead of trying to find a particular place to stop tomorrow, how about if we order up some lunches. Then we can just eat wherever and whenever we want."

Mom agrees. "You'd better order a box for each of us."

Given the tiny amount both parents have eaten on this trip, I think one box will most likely satisfy all of us, but I place the order and have directions to pick them up tomorrow morning after eight.

As we walk out of the restaurant, Mom suddenly remembers that Dad needs more stool softeners.

"I can run back to the store and get some," I volunteer. "It's not very far."

"No, you won't know what to look for." She doesn't trust me with such a task. "I'll pick some up tomorrow," she says.

At the bungalow, Mom recounts to Dad all the historical facts we learned this afternoon and the places we visited.

"They had some beautiful paintings in the museum, and we watched a very interesting film about the early years of Yellowstone."

While they talk, I settle into one of the green plastic chairs on our half of the porch and use the moment to reconnect with my own family and the real world. Unlike Yellowstone Lake, this village has clear cell phone service, and I'm able to reach Rob easily.

"Yeah, we had a good day. I took Elisabeth over for the two college interviews. I graded some papers while I waited. I even had time to take her home and have lunch before I had to take Clare to her violin lesson."

Although not necessarily complaining, his account of his day reminds me that this is no vacation for him either.

"Thanks for doing all of that," I say to Rob, missing him even more.

After I hang up, I watch the red sky colors fade over the hills and smell the wind grow colder. I knit four more rows on the Christmas mittens before retreating to the warm air inside.

As expected, we have no plans for an evening meal. I rummage through my bag for some trail mix. During our afternoon walk, Mom and I saw an advertisement for a slide show of Yellowstone's winter beauty set to original piano music.

"Do you mind if Mom and I go over to hear this, Dad?"

"No, not at all. I'm going to stay here and read my book." He taps the cover of one of the books I brought. He seems better rested and less agitated by his leg.

"Well, don't try to get up," Mom says. "There are some more granola bars in my bag if you get hungry."

Mom and I button up our coats and stroll over to Mammoth Springs' main lodge, specifically, to the Map Room. With full-length windows facing the town, the space spectacularly serves as the hotel's showcase meeting room for conferences or classes about Yellowstone. A hardwood floor waits to accommodate willing dancers. In addition to the two sofas at the front, brown straight-backed meeting chairs line up on the red-and-gold patterned carpet.

The room is impressive, not because of the dance floor or giant windows, but for what hangs on the north wall: a giant map of the United States made with fifteen types of wood from nine countries. Its massive ten-by-seventeen-foot frame dwarfs the rest of the furniture in the room. Not only does it outline political boundaries, the inlaid wood map also shows state capitals, major rivers, and other geographical detail.

Dad would love this grandiose display of fine craftsmanship. In retirement, he has acquired tools, patterns, and long planks of solid walnut and oak. He has built bookshelves, knickknack racks, coffee tables, side tables, and a clothes hamper for his children and grandchildren. For Mom and his own house, he has constructed a magazine rack, television hutch, and an assortment of shelving. More than one of the finished projects ended up as fuel for the stove, but most of them are quite beautiful just because he made them. I wish he could experience the majesty of this map tonight.

Mom and I settle into a table next to the windows on the opposite side of the map. From here, we continue our conversation about Dad, his cancer, my siblings, and the grandchildren. She asks about my plans when the kids are finished with high school. Eric still has six years before graduation, but I know that time will pass quickly. I honestly haven't considered what Rob and I will do once our schedules revolve around just us again.

The conversation turns to Rhonda's boys, Cory and Bryan. Bryan is going to college near Des Moines, and Cory is preparing to join the army next August. That makes us both a little nervous.

Rick, our entertainer for the evening, enters the room and loads a compact disc of piano ragtime. The only ragtime I know is Scott Joplin, but Mom recognizes this as a different composer. Rick stops by our table to draw the curtain and greet us. He is a former park concessions worker turned performer.

Mom asks him about the music playing through the speakers.

"Yes, you're right." His eyes light up in the presence of a fellow aficionado. They launch into a full discussion about the various types of ragtime. I have no idea what they're talking about, but given Mom's background, I shouldn't be surprised by what an impression she makes on this young man.

Mom was an established musician even in high school. On piano, she accompanied her school choir, played for dance studio practice, and for church. But she was best known for her alto voice in a high school girls' trio. Before graduating, the trio performed at hundreds of service organizations and public events held in Council Bluffs.

After receiving her teaching certificate, she taught fourth grade at several elementary schools, stopping when Rhonda was born. When she had a little more time, Mom attended music pedagogy classes in Omaha. She eventually cashed in her public school retirement money for a honey-colored Conover piano, charging a dollar-fifty for each thirty minute lesson. By the time she retired as a piano teacher more than thirty-five years later, she had taught the Minuet in G to more than two hundred students.

I recognize that my mother is a smart woman in general, but it was genius on her part to realize that she shouldn't teach her own children to play the piano. She paid money to have someone else do that. Even though she wasn't our formal teacher, her talent and love of music obviously flows through us. She often played sonatas, etudes, and scherzos long after we were in bed but not yet asleep. I wonder if she realized we memorized those songs, humming along as her fingers tamed the zebra keys.

Rick excuses himself from our table to begin the program. The room isn't crowded, but Yellowstone visitors fill each of the rows. Most are senior citizens, but I also see a group of young couples looking for things to do tonight. Several families with small children squeeze into the sofas near the front of the room.

Rick turns on his computer and projects his Yellowstone photographs onto a large screen in the front of the room. This week we have seen mountains and plains in spectacular autumn colors. I can't imagine the park any more beautiful, but Rick's photographs of the deep winter white coat show me another perspective of this exquisite landscape.

After the show, our entertainer engages us with a story about an encounter he had with a bear in a remote part of Yellowstone. He reveals more than one scar on his body as proof of his tale.

"I can't wait to tell Dad about this brown bear," I say, leaning over to Mom.

When we return to the cabin, though, Dad is the one with a story for us.

"Charles! What were you thinking?"

In our absence, Dad found the energy not only to shower but also shave and pull on a fresh set of new clothes.

"I even ate some of those pretzels Rin had in her bag," Dad says. "Like a bear foraging for some food." He chuckles, obviously pleased with himself.

I'm pleased, too.

Sunday

October 2

Yellowstone needs rain, and the weather certainly cooperates this morning. My shoes are muddy even though I tried to avoid puddles when I returned the room key and retrieved our box lunches. The rain is cold. It even smells cold.

Dad stands on the porch while Mom and I load the car. The less time he sits, the better.

"Bring that car closer, Rin," he orders through the rain. He doesn't want to drag his bum leg through the wet grass, plus he wants to keep his walker clean for this afternoon when he meets his navy friends. I want it to stay clean because it rides on top of our luggage in the trunk.

I have inched the car as close to the steps as possible without causing significant structural damage to the duplex on our other side, but it doesn't satisfy Dad.

"I can't, Dad. I can't maneuver the car in there any further. There isn't enough room."

"I could do it," he snaps under his breath.

A lucky break reduces the rain to a fine mist. As quickly as we can, we make for the car. The walker again doubles as a side rail for Dad as he shifts slowly down the steps onto the slick grass, grunting in rhythm with each movement. Once he is off the porch, he hobbles to the car door.

When I see Dad positioning himself into the vehicle, I take his walker and clean the stubs with some paper napkins and place it in the trunk. I slide behind the wheel and realize that Dad hasn't even clicked his seat belt yet.

This morning, Dad has trouble stretching far enough back in the seat to give his right leg sufficient room to swing in. Mom tries to help by pulling up on his trousers or gently lifting his leg from underneath. She knows exactly how much fine-tuning Dad can handle before he reaches his limit. Dad grimaces, moans, closes his eyes, and does whatever he can to exhale the pain that pulses through his entire leg. Gently but firmly, Mom shifts his right foot up, past the door ledge, and onto the floor of the car. Dad makes a final adjustment and then lets out a long sigh of relief, set until our next stop.

We are headed to the West Yellowstone entrance, about forty-five miles south. We're not even three miles from the geothermal wonders of Mammoth Springs when heavy, thick raindrops splatter on the windshield.

"Is that snow on that hill or just frost?" I point across the valley to our left. Flakes begin to fall against the windows, answering my question.

The Mammoth to Madison road weaves and turns in the high altitudes. No barriers prevent us from missing a curve and becoming human pumpkins down a ravine. Snow quickly covers the highway, and I can't see where the pavement ends and the cliff begins.

The white blanket also grows over the hills, muting the colors of the bushes and grass that were so vivid yesterday. Normally, the beauty of this scene would calm me, even call me to play in the dancing flakes. Driving in the snow, with deep gullies on either side of the road, however, is not at all relaxing or entertaining.

I'm uncomfortable inside the car, too. My increased adrenaline keeps me plenty warm, but Dad, with his undershirt, plaid flannel shirt, and thick pullover sweater, is shivering. I move the vents to blow toward him and away from my face, but that doesn't keep my eyes from drying out. We've been driving an hour already and are still inside the park boundaries.

My hands firmly grip the ten and two o'clock position of the steering wheel. A van ahead of us gives me some perspective and makes it easier to see the road.

"I'm glad this guy is making tracks for us," I mention. Just then, the van misses the curve and skids off the side of the road in slow motion. Having reached a plateau in the terrain, the vehicle glides safely to a stop. None of us speak or react outwardly, but I can feel myself shaking inside. I lift my foot off the accelerator and cautiously coast past the van.

From my rearview mirror, I watch the driver coax his vehicle back onto the road. Now it's my turn to make the first path in the snow. Mom and Dad, keeping very quiet during this whole ride, have never been more alert since we left home.

"These are big flakes," Dad comments. "That means it will stop pretty soon." He tries to instill confidence in me.

After another hour, we reach a much lower elevation and much more amiable climate. Dad was right. The snow subsides as we drive away from the ominous clouds still hovering over the Yellowstone Mountains.

Before we leave the park completely, but before entering Idaho, we cross into a slender slip of Montana.

"Four states," I say to Dad, believing this to be a fairly significant accomplishment for us.

"Mom, will you call Rob and ask him if we are going to run into any more precipitation today?"

Rob loves all things concerned with weather. He knows the names of the reporters on the television weather channel. He tracks approaching storms from the west coast, and checks our home temperature every morning before retrieving the newspaper. Today he uses the Internet to provide us with an updated forecast.

"The map shows clear skies to the west of the park, so you should be good." Mom relays Rob's words to me, but in my mind I hear him reporting in the same style as his weather-channel friends.

"But it looks like it's snowing pretty good now in Yellowstone right down to Pocatello. I'll bet you're glad you didn't have to drive through that."

I want Mom to tell him that we *did* just drive through that, but she describes our last few hours to Rob as if it were a regular morning commute.

With no bad weather to delay us, we set our course for Sun Valley in western Idaho. Here we will meet up with other sailors from around the United States for a navy reunion, the central purpose for our trip.

Four years after he had witnessed the drowning of his brother and brother-in-law, Dad was restless. He needed independence and craved his own experiences. He wanted to see the world, and the U.S. Navy was his ticket. Not knowing how his parents would react, he waited to tell them about his decision until after he had sealed his contract with the military.

Dad served as a seaman aboard the USS *Passumpsic* from 1952 to 1956. His designation was Fire Control Technician Striker, a distinctly unglamorous but necessary service aboard a tanker ship. He performed menial tasks with his fellow sailors, joined them in endless card games of pitch, and shared together sad letters and unbelievable yarns from home. Four or five of his shipmates kept in contact with Dad after leaving the boat, but most he never saw again—until ten years ago.

The first *Passumpsic* reunion was held in 1995. Each year the sailors congregate at a different location around the country. Mom and Dad even hosted one of the reunions in Council Bluffs with fellow shipmate Bud Ferrell and his wife, Artis. The reunions are open to sailors of all ages, genders, and ranks. It's like a family reunion without the inconvenience of being related.

When Dad dressed this morning, he packed away his regular hat in the suitcase. He now dons a navy blue cap with an outline of the actual ship stitched in white across the front, the words "USS *Passumpsic*" embroidered in yellow above the boat, and "*AO-107*" written in the same color below. Anxious to see his friends again, the driving today seems extra tedious for him.

Midway to the resort, we watch for the boundaries of Craters of the Moon National Monument. Rob suggested in the phone conversation that we stop here.

"It's supposed to be pretty cool." In addition to his weather interests, he is also fascinated with all things lunar.

Although a sign tells us we have entered the boundaries of the park, we can't discern any distinct signs or changes in the terrain. The scenery is as flat, dusty, and filled with sagebrush as the previous hour's landscape. In the distance, three or four dark mounds might be considered "craters" if I use my imagination.

"I don't see anything here, do you?" I ask my equally unimpressed passengers.

An overlook further along the highway provides a better perspective of the horizon. Admittedly, more black heaps grow in the distance, but as a whole this national monument is anticlimactic.

"I think we should go on through," I suggest. But immediately before the monument headquarters, a green sign with white writing captures our attention, the type of sign we have been seeking this entire trip.

"Driving Tour."

At last, a national park created with tourists just like us in mind. I barely slow down in time to turn left into the entrance. Excited by what adventure might be ahead, I pass by the visitor's center rather than stopping for historical perspective as we have done for every other park on this trip. Gleefully, we head straight for the toll hut.

I show my national park pass to a man wearing the same sage green uniform as the rangers in Teton and Yellowstone. The exception is that this ranger wears a matching green earring.

"Enjoy your visit," he says as he hands us a park brochure and map.

Before the car can shift into second gear, Dad abruptly puts a stop to my enthusiasm.

"I've got to use the can," Dad says with a hint of desperation in his voice.

"Why didn't you say earlier?" I ask, addressing him the way an exasperated parent speaks to a toddler. "We just passed the visitor's center. We could have stopped there."

"I thought you were going to stop. We usually stop at those places," he says defensively.

Up ahead is a closed-for-the-season campground with a rustic lavatory that appears to have plumbing still functioning this late into the season. I park the car directly in front of the bathrooms, not worried that anyone else might need to visit the facilities.

As we are here, I decide to visit to the ladies' side. I hand over the walker to Mom who helps Dad wrestle out of the car. In the time it takes me to use the bathroom, wash my hands, and comb my hair, Dad is just now reaching the restroom door.

Mom wants to take advantage of the stop as well but makes sure I understand what is happening before she leaves.

"He'll knock on the door when he is finished to signal us to open it for him," she instructs.

Engrossed in reading the park brochure, I hear but don't bother to answer.

"Are you listening?"

"Yes," I say, embarrassed that she had to ask me twice but also frustrated that after four days together, she doesn't trust me to know how to help Dad.

We finish up at the rest area and begin our official tour. Craters of the Moon National Monument may be a national park, but it is nothing like the parks we have just seen. Instead of beautiful and picturesque landscape, the earth here is pitch black, clumpy, and jagged. It appears shiny and wet, but it's actually dry. Mom gives us more background.

"According to this," she waves the brochure at us from the backseat, "this isn't rock. It's lava."

"Lava?" Dad is suspicious.

"That's what it says," Mom defends herself. "No volcano or anything, just lava that seeped through the earth and dried this way."

The park brochure itself describes the formations as "weird."

We stop at the first overlook.

"I wonder how many science fiction movies they make here," Dad ponders.

They all should be, I think to myself.

"Man, I'd hate to be a park ranger with this assignment," Dad says, soaking in the unusual terrain.

"It wouldn't be so bad," I retort. "I'm sure there are worse locations." My mind draws a blank for supporting examples.

"Well, I hope they get rotated around a little," he says with sympathy. "It's the pits."

At the second overlook, I pull into a space with an expansive view of the park below, providing a dramatic backdrop for our lunch. We'll be warm enough in the car even though we can feel the wind whipping against it.

I retrieve our boxes from the trunk and pass them out. While I devour my lunch, Mom and Dad only pick at theirs. With my thin, white, plastic knife, I peel one of the apples and then slice it in thin sections. Despite my attempts to make fruit easier to eat, Dad prefers the peaches inside a small plastic container with a peel-off lid.

We finish the drive through the park but remain puzzled by the strange, unfamiliar territory that seems to be mocking us. Despite its quirky appearance, we develop a fondness for the area and leave with a genuine appreciation of this very odd natural phenomenon, this park with a sense of humor.

For the next hour we enjoy a broad and expansive horizon where tumbleweeds, withered sunflowers, heather, and sage weave together new patterns and textures. The plains then turn to heavily forested mountains as we turn north on the road to Sun Valley.

"These are beautiful," I say of the southern Sawtooth Mountain Range of Idaho. "I would love to see the view from the top."

"And roll a pumpkin off 'er, too," Dad adds.

By midafternoon, we reach Ketchum, the town where our resort is located. A sign points the way to the resort, and we follow the directions.

Sun Valley is a long-established American ski resort designed to resemble a traditional European mountain village and attract wealthy guests. A human-faced sun glowing beside the words "Sun Valley" serves as its logo. Beneath the old Alpine lettering, we learn that this is "America's First and Finest All Seasons Resort."

One of the tri-fold pamphlets Mom received in their reunion packet boasts that Sun Valley has hosted celebrity guests such as Clark Gable, Errol Flynn, Claudette Colbert, Bing Crosby, and Gary Cooper. In addition to skiing the local mountain, visitors are invited to shop at trendy clothing and chocolate stores in the village by day and enjoy shows starring high-profile skaters at the glamorous ice rink by night.

But October is the season between seasons when chair lifts are pulled down for maintenance, businesses are locked tight, and the temperatures aren't cold enough to sustain the ice rink. The great advantage of being here during the "off season," though, is paying the "off season" room rates.

"It says here we have to register at the Sun Valley Lodge," Mom reads from one of the reunion letters.

In addition to condominiums, private residences, and other more secluded accommodations, Sun Valley has two massive hotels on the property, one identified as a lodge and the other as an inn, with hundreds of rooms in each. Squinting, I try to find a sign that directs us to our assigned location.

Conveniently, I see signs for the lodge and park the car directly in front of the entrance. This time it's Mom, not me, who checks us into the hotel. Even though this is Dad's reunion, she is the one who has made the arrangements for this part of the trip. With her purse in one hand and the confirmation papers clutched in the other, she climbs out of the backseat and walks through the big double glass doors of the hotel lobby. Dad and I pass the time in the LeSabre watching for other cars and potential navy reunion attendees.

In less than two minutes, Mom returns with frustration marked on her face. With defenses on full alert, she sits back in the car and slams the door shut.

"Well, they'd better get some people who speak English around here, or they aren't going to be in business very long."

I can't figure out what went wrong, but I don't ask for details.

"We need to get to a place where I can show you where we need to go," she insists.

"Okay," I say, even though I don't understand what she wants me to do. "Should I go back to the main road?"

"No. You need to pull *over* so I can *show* you."

I comply immediately.

"We are here." Her right index finger stabs the miniature town on the map. "We have to go past the filling station to get to the inn." She swipes her finger furiously along the pretend road and then hands me the folded paper to work out the details.

According to the layout, and by looking out the front window of the car, I can see the inn is just across the parking lot. Nonetheless, without question, I use the route instructed by my mother. I can't figure out why she is so rattled by all of this.

A circular drive curves in front of the inn, and again, I find a space directly in front of another set of glass double doors. After she removes the clutter from her lap, Mom marches inside on her continued quest to find us our room.

This time Dad sleeps while we wait. I find another pamphlet to read and scout the area for out-of-state license plates. Mom must be finding success because she has been inside for ten minutes.

When she does return, she walks to Dad's side of the car and speaks sharply through his open window.

"If these people don't get someone who can speak English," she begins with a big breath.

Dad's oncologist is from India. I've never met him but I have no reason to doubt his competency as a doctor. Still, his heavy accent coupled with my father's advanced hearing loss make the physician's words nearly impossible to understand. My parents listen closely and patiently to their medical professional because they need to know what is being said.

Today, Mom's patience is thin, and she is tired of straining to understand unknown words and strange circumstances. She longs for familiar sounds, for a familiar life.

"Okay, Mom," I say, leaning over Dad to talk to her through the lowered window. "Where is it we go?"

"I'm not sure." She sounds nearly defeated. "The receptionist told me to go in that door, but that's not right. I don't think she told me right. When I asked if it was handicapped accessible, she asked me what that meant, so I just gave up."

"You and Rin go check it out," Dad instructs, just as he has done every other time we have arrived at new lodgings.

I park the car in a more permanent spot and in a place Dad won't be disturbed by the glare of the sun. Mom and I go in search of our room.

Entering through more tall glass doors, we wind our way back to the main entrance. This lobby is different from that of the Idaho Falls Comfort Inn or of any of our accommodations in the national parks. Chandeliers hang from the ceiling and appear even larger when reflected in the wall of massive mirrors. I'm completely impressed by the enormous flower display on the round wooden table, wondering if the stems are real. The hallways, decorated with flocked wallpaper, are a veritable maze of subhalls and ramps that have no apparent purpose. We turn right, and then left, down more ramps, then finally discover our assigned room.

Like the juxtaposition in lobbies, I anticipate a stark contrast between the rooms where we have slept the last four nights and what is behind Door Number 36. I don't have to open the door too wide to confirm my hypothesis.

Floral mauve and yellow drapes match the bedspread and coordinate with the striped wallpaper. Queen Anne chairs surround a glass-top table. A plasma television mounted on the wall provides full cable access. Movies are extra. A giant mahogany armoire hides a room refrigerator, extremely convenient for guests like us traveling with our own food, and a safe. We won't need the safe, but we will use the brass cans for our trash.

A double dressing sink made of marble stands between the bathroom and the closet with mirrored doors. Thick white terry-cloth robes hang inside the bathroom. To my dismay, a glorious, gleaming white soaking tub with silver fixtures waits to refresh any weary guest, or at least any guest who is able to lift a limb high enough to climb into it.

While an outside exit is directly adjacent to our room, two steps immediately outside of the door complicate the path to the sidewalk. Also, the walk to the parking lot is a fair distance. Even if Dad could manage the curb up to the sidewalk or the steps to the building, no parking places are nearby. Dad couldn't possibly trek the same path Mom and I just covered. Finally, the hospitality suite for the reunion events is on the opposite side of the lobby. This room is impractical for Dad in every way.

Mom and I return to the reception desk where I meet the woman whose accent caused Mom so much aggravation. The clerk is neither abrasive nor assertive, but clearly English is not her native language. This soft-spoken woman in her early twenties is dressed in a white shirt, black pants, and black vest. Her accent suggests Italy, but she wears no nametag to identify her homeland. She sympathizes with the worried creases growing deeper on Mom's forehead.

"I look for something, but I not see." Like me, Mom didn't request a handicapped room because at the time she made the reservations, Dad didn't need one.

"No closer room," apologizes the clerk.

Thirty minutes have elapsed since we left Dad waiting in the car.

"Mom, why don't you go let Dad know what's happening. I'll get something figured out."

She agrees and starts toward the doors but then turns around, uncertain as to which is the correct exit. She discreetly returns to the desk to wait with me.

We three women stand silently at the hotel desk, listening to the computer keys clicking for an alternative to our assigned room.

"Hmm." The woman shakes her head negatively.

"Do you have a wheelchair that we could use while we stay here?" Mom suggests an ideal solution.

The receptionist's expression changes immediately.

"Yes! We have!" She lifts the phone receiver and orders a wheelchair be delivered to Room 36.

"No, no. That's no good," Mom brusquely objects. "We still have to get him to the room. We need the wheelchair *here*."

As if he heard her command, a man wearing the same black hotel uniform as the clerk emerges from an invisible door behind the desk and wheels the chair toward us. With this new gift, Mom and I retrace our steps back to Dad, past the mirrors, the chandeliers, and the gorgeous floral centerpiece.

When Dad sees us with the wheelchair he is hostile.

"I don't want that thing," he says in disgust. "I want to walk for awhile."

I understand that his legs crave to stretch out and be employed, but I also suspect he doesn't want his friends seeing him in a wheelchair. What Dad doesn't realize, though, is that these corridors are long and require that he walk more than five steps to reach the room.

"It's pretty far, Charles," Mom warns. "I don't think you can make it all the way."

"Well, I'll walk as far as I can then," he snaps. The mounting tension increases the urgency for us to find our room and relax.

With one of the smaller bags in my left hand, I open the door to the hotel for Dad and his walker to pass through. He stops to rest and reconnoiter down the endless corridors as I explain the series of turns we have to navigate before we reach the room. Mom follows behind with the wheelchair. We go no further than the ornate flower arrangement before he succumbs.

"Okay. I guess I'd better have it then," he says to Mom.

While Dad stands with his weight on his left foot, Mom slowly rolls the chair up to the back of his leg without actually touching it. She pulls the brake handle into place to prevent the chair from shifting, and Dad eases into the seat as gently as possible.

After pausing for a breath, he puts his left foot on the steel plate where it rests. When he attempts to lift his right foot to match, it doesn't reach. The footrest is higher than the chair he uses at home and even higher than the ones in the airport. He tries three more times, and even Mom tries to lift it without success.

We try to manually adjust the plate. While I hold Dad's foot out of the way, Mom kneels at the base of the chair and attempts to jiggle it down.

"I wish I had my pliers on me," Dad says seriously. Mom continues to fumble with the footrest when a man of about sixty and his similarly aged wife approach Dad.

"Hello, Sailor," the man says. They haven't met before, but the new friend recognizes Dad by his *Passumpsic* hat.

Dad introduces himself, his wife, struggling to perform engineering reconstruction on the chair, and his daughter, protecting her father's foot in her cupped hands.

"Hello," I manage without removing my hands or getting off the floor. Mom, however, doesn't hesitate to stand erect to make her greeting.

"Hi, I'm Zola," she volunteers. She pulls herself together in a flash, careful not to reveal any irritation about our current situation.

"Do you think we are in the right place?" asks the man.

"We think we are," says Mom, "although we haven't seen anyone else yet. But we just arrived."

After informal banter about when they served on the ship and in what capacity, the navy couple's attention is drawn back to me kneeling and supporting Dad's foot. They recognize that this might be an awkward time and excuse themselves, promising to meet Mom and Dad later at the reception.

Our brief interruption didn't resolve the original problem. The footplates will not budge. Because we are unable to make adjustments, Dad's very tender and painful foot is left to dangle precariously close to the floor. If his foot should happen to scrape the floor, the chair will continue to roll forward over his limb.

Knowing the risks, Dad holds his foot off the ground clutching the leg of his jeans. Mom, still energized with emotion, insists that she be the one to push Dad's chair while the walker lies across the armrests. She wraps her bony and bent fingers around the rubber handlebars, and the veins on the back of her frail hands show through her thin and spotty skin. She needs every bit of her strength to move Dad forward.

Although her grip is strong, her shoes betray her. The soles are too slick against the carpet to maintain any traction. When she starts down one of the long ramps, the chair gains momentum and pulls her along with it.

I skitter ahead on Mom's left, grab the armrest, and pull against it like the reigns of a runaway horse. Mom has no choice but to allow me to push the chair to the room. She refuses to surrender all control, however, and holds on to the left armrest in an attempt to steer it to the room. This actually makes it more difficult for me because her weight upsets the balance and forces the wheels either into the wall or over her feet.

Two ramps and as many corners later, we finally arrive at our room, open the door, and move Dad inside. The room thermometer reads seventy-five degrees Fahrenheit.

"Let's get some heat in here," Dad calls out.

He unfolds his walker, lifts himself out of the chair, and limps immediately to the bed located the furthest from the door and bathroom. He struggles with the blankets but eventually lets out his notorious moan to announce he is now comfortable and settled under the covers. He is fully clothed, including shoes in case his swollen foot won't fit back in.

I move the car around to the back of the building where I can more easily unload our gear. After everything is in the room, I search for a reason to leave the hotel, certain that Mom and Dad would like their privacy as well.

"Hey, I need to do some laundry," I say. A hotel portfolio lists several cleaning choices. As I consider my options, the telephone on the table rings. Bud and Artis, Mom and Dad's navy friends from Council Bluffs, want to confirm we have arrived safely. They drove from Iowa, across the roads Dad wanted to use, without any daughter in tow.

"Sure, sure. Come on over." My mother's lilting voice on the phone conceals from the world any frustrations she feels.

"I'll meet you in the lobby because you'll never figure out how to get back to this room."

Mom hangs up.

"Do you want me to go meet them, Mom?" Although I'm not certain I'll find my way back either.

"No, I will get them," she says, determined to learn the secrets of the hotel hallways. She carefully notes the number of corners, the direction of the turns, and any other signs that will help her memorize the path to the front desk.

In less time than I expect, Mom proudly arrives back at the room with Bud and Artis.

Artis is a gray-haired but vibrant woman in her seventies, wears a knee-length skirt and comfortable sweater. She was recently ordained an Episcopalian minister.

Burly with a full beard on his lower face and chin, Bud is not unlike the bears we have been seeking, except for the bald spot on top of his head. He tries to convince me he is as rough as Artis is gentle. Eyeglasses that are too large for his face slide down his nose. With a full girth around the middle, he uses suspenders rather than a belt to hold up his jeans.

"Which one is this?" he asks Dad about me in mock intimidation.

"This is Renae," Dad introduces me. "She's our third one."

"Renae? You don't look like a 'Renae.' You look like a 'Gloria.'"

Too tired to defend my identity, I let it pass, believing it must be a form of navy humor. Also, because Dad's spirits improved immediately when his friend walked through the door, I quickly warm to Bud and his wife.

"You're the lawyer, huh?" Bud asks me. I proceed cautiously, but before I can deflect the question, he launches into his repertoire of lawyer jokes. Bud drives a school bus, but I don't know any retaliatory bus driver humor.

"Everything is so expensive," Artis says to Mom. "It costs sixty-four dollars for the barbeque." a western-themed dinner is scheduled for tomorrow night.

"I'm not spending that," Mom says defiantly.

"Oh, but you're only here once." Artis tries to coax Mom and Dad despite her own reservations about the cost.

Mom is not persuaded. "Yes, I'm only here once, but I don't have to pay that kind of money for food."

"You guys keep talking," I say. "I was just about to go into Ketchum and do laundry."

"Okay, Gloria, have fun with that."

I'm not sure how long I'll be gone, and I don't want Dad to miss the opening reception.

"If I'm not back in time, would you be able to help Dad get down to the hospitality room tonight?"

"Oh, yes," Artis replies, happy to be useful.

"I asked at the desk where the reception was going to be," Mom says. "They just pointed me to another room, but that was the restaurant. I have no idea where it is."

"Oh, yes. You have to go through the restaurant," Artis tells her.

"Don't worry, Gloria," Bud's voice booms. "We'll get 'em there."

With a phone book map to guide me, I return to Ketchum. Before Bud and Artis arrived, Mom asked me to find stool softeners for Dad, a task she wouldn't give me in Mammoth. She no longer has a choice and explicitly described the over-the-counter medication, right down to the color and size of the outside packaging.

"Do you understand what to get?" she asked me.

I think so.

A locally owned drugstore is on one of the main streets in town. I quickly find the Senokot, the exact medicine Mom instructed me to purchase. My pride in finding the right bottle quickly fades as I face the myriad of options for this particular brand.

A regular version is available in boxes of 20, 50, and 100 tablets. Packaged in a different color with the letter *S* across the side is a formula with an extra dose of stool softener, available in 10, 30, and 60 tablets. The store also stocks a package with a green label to indicate double strength. This is the "XTRA" version, offered in sizes of either 12 or 36 tablets.

After my conversation with Mom about remembering the right medication, I can't return to the hotel with the wrong stuff. The *S* seems familiar, and I quickly purchase thirty tablets of the medicine.

A Suds and Duds is in the same neighborhood as the pharmacy, and I unload our ripening clothes. After I feed two machines with soap and quarters, I call home, hoping to find sympathy from Rob.

"No, he's not here," Eric tells me. "He's getting Clare from her soccer game."

"Wait a minute," I say. "Elisabeth was supposed to take her to her game." I set up this arrangement before I left.

"Well, Elisabeth took her, but she didn't stay for the game. She says she only had directions to *take* Clare, not bring her home."

Elisabeth. Obviously, the expectation was for her to take her younger sister to the game, wait for her, and then bring her home. But I'm not there to sort it out.

"Oh, and Mom, I had a bad soccer game today because the coach said anyone who didn't show up at practice wouldn't get to play, and because I missed practice Thursday because of that violin concert you made us go to, I only got to play about fifteen minutes."

I was seeking sympathy from my spouse but find myself trying to console my son. I apologize to Eric for making him attend the concert.

"I'll talk to Dad later." I press the red button on my phone to end the call.

After what appear to be some sort of mechanical seizure, the wash cycle ends. I pull the wet shirts, socks, and jeans out of the washer and into a wire cart and then roll the clothes over to the dryer. The drone of the huge machine becomes hypnotic and calms me while I read my book. By the time I fold the laundry and place it neatly into my bag, most of my tension has evaporated into the warm moist air of the Laundromat.

I make a stop at a nearby convenience store for a quart of milk, string cheese, tomato and orange juice. No bananas. I also buy plastic spoons, forks, and knives, all of which will allow us to eat more cheaply in our expensive hotel room.

When I return to the hotel, the housekeeping staff has already turned down our sheets and placed chocolates on our pillows. The dairy products fit easily into the mini fridge, and I lay the clean laundry into the drawers of a beautiful dark-wood dresser. Mom and Dad are still at the reception. On the glass table is a note from Artis with an invitation to join them in the Ram Room when I am ready.

I linger in the room as long as I dare before I eventually make my way to the hospitality suite. There I find Mom guarding Dad's wheelchair but no Dad. He uses his walker to move amongst his friends. Once he sees me in the room, however, he finishes his conversation and slowly works his way back to Mom and me.

"Do you want to get something to eat?" Mom invites. The Craters of the Moon lunch was a long time ago, but I can see that both of them are anxious to get back to the room. They have yet to experience the same luxurious solitude that I found in the Laundromat.

"No, that's fine," I say, remembering I can always dig into the cache of groceries stocked in the mini fridge.

We help Dad back into the chair, and I notice that the footrest has been adjusted.

"Yes," Mom says. "On the way here, we stopped at the desk to see if it could be fixed. The man who brought it out to us had the right tools and snap-snap, got it to work."

With his walker folded across the armrests, I check that I'm not making marks on the walls. The inexplicably steep inclines continue to baffle me, and I note that a wheelchair is infinitely easier to control on wood, concrete, or marble than on carpet. The chair has a mind of its own and wants to either roll away from me or on top of Mom's toes.

When we finally reach the room, Dad sits in a chair by the table rather than lay flat on the bed, as I had expected he would do. I proudly trot out the purchases I made, including vegetable juice rather than crunchy vegetables that would break their teeth. Every day I learn a little more about their needs. Mom also tells me what a good job I did finding the right medication for Dad.

As I split a can of juice with my father I revisit the barbeque reservations.

"I know that the dinner tomorrow night seems expensive, but you've gone to all this effort to be here for the reunion; you shouldn't miss anything. You should go to as many of these things as you can and not worry about the cost. The real cost was getting here." I meant both financially and physically.

"Well, it's just too much for a dinner." Mom's mind is convinced, and Dad fully agrees.

"You know," I try to persuade, "if it only cost half this amount, you would go, wouldn't you?" They wait for me to finish my argument. "So really, this is over sixteen dollars?"

"Oh, no," Mom neighs. "It's a whole lot more than sixteen dollars."

"Yes, you're right. For all three of us, the total cost is close to a hundred dollars. But if it was fifty dollars for all of us to go, I'm guessing you wouldn't hesitate. It's more than we are used to paying for a meal, but might it be worth a splurge this time?"

"It's not the money," Dad says.

I know it is the money.

He continues. "It's because it's so far away from here, away from the hotel. It's such a hassle."

"Dad, you know I'll take you. You have already come over fifteen hundred miles to be here. You drove through Yellowstone. You only need to go a half of a mile down the road to get to the dinner." He's still not convinced.

I moan inside my head and drop the subject.

With Mom's assistance, Dad brushes his teeth, takes his medicine, and removes his shoes before finally settling under the blankets for the night.

"Bring me my book, will ya, Ma." Mom finds one of the biographies I brought along especially for Dad and hands it to him. She then snuggles down on my bed where she explores the numerous cable channels at the flick of a thumb.

I monopolize the glass table with my laptop, typing as much for therapy as for note taking.

"You aren't trying to use e-mail from here, are you?" Mom inquires suspiciously. I hadn't considered it, but now that she brings it up, it might be a good distraction. I leaf through the hotel brochure with instructions on how to use the Internet.

"It looks like I can tap into the hotel line. There may be a fifty-cent charge for outgoing calls, but I'm not sure."

"Better not take the chance then," Mom warns.

"Plus tax," Dad adds.

I am willing to risk a half a dollar in order to make contact with the outside world, but I don't bother. Rob would be asleep anyway.

"The movies here are eleven dollars," Mom says. "I'm not going to get caught watching that." She finds a public television special about the Mayan ruins instead.

Within minutes, both she and Dad are asleep.

Occasionally, I slip into the bedrooms of my slumbering teenagers just to see the innocence of their faces. I have the same feelings for my parents tonight as I look at the tired lines around their eyes. Whenever I see my children in this way, and seeing my parents sleeping tonight, all the tension of the day washes away, just like the sound of the dryers at the Laundromat. Everything is in perspective.

Monday

October 3

Cold rain rolls down our windows this morning, forcing me onto the hotel treadmill for my morning walk. Later today we'll drive through parts of the Sawtooth National Forest and Recreational Area. I want to move around as much as possible before spending so much time on the tour bus.

The exercise allows me to catch up with news in the world that otherwise disappears whenever I take any vacation. The events outside of our immediate location seem distant, even irrelevant. I have no interest in anything the television news personalities say this morning.

After pacing off three miles, I return to the room for a shower and breakfast, which includes a few of my purchases from last night. Even after I finish eating, we still have an hour before we're scheduled to meet the rest of the group.

I sit pretzel-legged on my hastily made bed and knit a few more rows on Clare's Christmas scarf. Dad is fully dressed but stays submerged under the covers to ward off the chill. Bud and Artis, also ahead of schedule, join us in our room for conversation.

Bud swelters in the heat of the room despite his short sleeves. He balances awkwardly on the edge of the Queen Anne chair next to the media cabinet. Mom and Artis discuss plans for the day.

"So, have you decided about tonight, Zola?" Artis asks about the barbeque. I unravel more yarn and pretend to be interested only in the tension of my stitches.

"Well, I think we'll go," Mom answers as if it is a matter of fact. "After all, we've already paid for it."

They've changed their minds?

The conversation jumps to another topic before I have a chance to clarify. The two couples remember old friends attending the reunion as well friends who are absent, speculating on the reason for the nonappearances.

The topic abruptly turns to politics, specifically, the invasion of Iraq by the United States. Bud, Artis, and Mom are deep in their discussion when Dad's voice emerges from underneath the blankets.

"You know, I don't agree with everything this president has done. But I think one thing George Bush has done a great deal for is to push back the terrorist threat to this country."

On this point, I couldn't disagree more with my father, but I stay silent and continue to knit at a steady pace. At Thanksgiving or any other holiday gatherings, our family has the good sense to avoid subjects related to international trade, capital punishment, and gun control. It seems uncharacteristic for Dad to interject now, especially when no one expected him to participate in the conversation at all.

The four of them continue a discourse of other current events until a lull in the conversation creates a quiet awkwardness in the room.

"Aaaaaaaaaarrrrrrp."

Without warning, the silence is breached by a groan from the depths of Bud's soul. The air released from across the room is far louder and cruder than any outburst my father has produced on this trip. Dad, who is buried in blankets up to his chin, opens his eyes widely when he hears the primeval noise. He turns his head toward me with a grin spread across his face.

Dad feels sufficiently rested, and we run out of topics for conversation. We decide it's time to meet the others for our outing today. The five of us parade down the corridors of the hotel to the other side of the hotel. I push Dad in his wheelchair and Mom follows. Bud and Artis bring up the rear.

As Mom learned last night, we have to go through a restaurant area in order to reach the meeting room.

"Well, see that door over there?" a waiter at the restaurant this morning points across to the far end of the room. "You can get in that way." He then disappears with a tray of dirty dishes.

I thread Dad's wheelchair in and out of the tables only to discover that the portal to the reception room is locked.

"Excuse me," I ask another waiter. "We're trying to get to the Ram Room, but this door is locked."

"Oh, sure," the second waiter responds. "You can go through the kitchen."

An unusual alternative, but without any other option, we form our queue again and meander through the kitchen, this time dodging the iceberg lettuce and chef knives. We reach the back door only to find it locked as well. Laughter from the other side of the wall is muffled but hearty. No doubt the reunion attendees entered the Ram Room from the outside approach, the one with the five steps leading up to the front doors.

"Hey!" Bud bellows through the wall. "Hey! Somebody needs to open this door!"

The sailors hear Bud's voice and eventually realize he isn't joking. The latch to the door is found, and we make our aberrant entrance into the reception room.

Most of the men in the room are wearing navy blue baseball-style caps exactly like the one sitting on my father's head. In addition to the name of the boat emblazoned across the front, miniature gold ships are pinned to the caps, one for each reunion the sailors have attended.

Of the fifty or so people at this reunion, less than half ever set foot on the *Passumpsic*. The others are spouses, friends, or extended family like myself. An official photographer and his wife also join the group. Mom says he has been to every reunion this crew has organized.

The *Passumpsic* was an oil tanker named for the Passumpsic River in Vermont. Commissioned in 1946, it swam mostly in far eastern Asian waters. In 1964, the ship underwent major renovations to increase its length and cargo capacity and as a result was "jumbo-ized." The seamen separate themselves into groups according to whether service was before or after jumbo-ization. By 1973, the *Passumpsic* officially ended its service, and the last rumors were that it now sits near Karachi, Pakistan, after being sold as scrap metal in 1991.

The sailors in the room are tall, short, skinny, well rounded, graying, bald, and except for a Native American from Arizona, appear to all be pale-skinned. Although I'm told that women served aboard the ship in the later years, the military personnel at this reunion are exclusively male.

The ages of the attendees also reflect the life span of the ship, from Korea to Vietnam. Of the servicemen present, only a handful served on the ship at the same time. Five or six of them are twenty years younger than Dad and Bud. Many are meeting today for the first time. I observe their behaviors and eavesdrop on their conversations, curious to know their motivation for wanting to be a part of this gathering. Specifically, I want to learn what about this group compels a dying man to expend his last reservoir of energy to be here.

While we wait for the bus to arrive, I study the photographs of celebrities lining the party room walls. A framed print of Lucille Ball skiing with her two children is my favorite. Only when I run out of pictures of famous people on these mountains do I look out the window to the real world to see large white flakes falling from the sky.

Word arrives at the Ram Room that the bus can't pull up as close as we thought.

"We need everyone to just walk over to the bus stop," one of the reunion organizers explains. "Just go out these doors, and the bus stop is only about two blocks away." He points us in the direction of the bus.

Mom and I exchange glances, knowing two blocks for us means two blocks plus a return hike through the kitchen, restaurant, and hotel lobby, and then finally pushing the wheelchair through the wet snow.

"Take me over to those steps, Rin," Dad directs me quietly.

I look over to the five steps that lead directly to the outside door and sidewalk, the same steps that were too many for us to use in the first place.

Like a magnet, the rest of the navy crew is naturally drawn toward Dad. He is wary of the steps, but he hears his friends calling out words of support.

"We'll help you, Charles," says one.

"We won't let you fall," from another.

Dad lifts the walker off of his lap and sets it up in front of him. I pull the wheelchair away from his foot slowly until his weight fully balances on the walker. Then he inches over to the steps.

"Here you go, Charles," one of the men says. "Put your hand on my shoulder." To my astonishment, Dad abandons his walker. He grips the stair railing with his right hand and steadies his left hand on the shoulder of a friend.

Very deliberately, Dad steps down with his left foot, using his right one first for balance and then drags it down to catch the other limb. He repeats this meticulous demonstration four more times until he reaches the bottom and we release a collective sigh of relief. Bud grabs the walker from my hands before I have a chance to absorb what has just happened.

"Let me take that for you." Without waiting for my response, someone scoops up the wheelchair from under my grasp and carries it outside.

From atop of the landing, I watch this group of aging men, acquaintances more than friends, find a way to move down these impossible steps together. Dad didn't request help, and no one actually offered any. The supporting arms just appeared.

Dad's motivation for being here begins to come into focus.

Our bus is a comfortable, typical vehicle used for sightseeing, complete with a pair of blue and red upholstered seats riding high on each side. Wide glass windows provide an unobstructed view of the mountains. Dad manages the three steps to board the bus with relative ease. Ascending requires less of his sense of balance than descending. For each step, he only has to place his left leg on the first step, and with his arms gripping the two handrails, pull his right one up next to his left foot. Mom boards directly after him, and they occupy the front seats saved just for them.

The bus driver helps me stash the wheelchair in the cargo area below, and I place the folded walker on the bus behind the driver, across from Mom and Dad. Three people offer to give up their seats for me to be able to sit close to Mom and Dad. While grateful for their generosity, I decline, hoping instead to find privacy and quiet further back.

Artis and Bud are already on the bus, and a seat is open near them. Even though I was looking forward to time alone, I like Mom and Dad's friends, and I'll enjoy being with them.

"Look, it's Gloria coming back here to sit with us," Bud broadcasts to his fellow passengers. I tuck into the seat and move next to a window with a good view of the mountains.

Our first destination is Hailey, a town of about six thousand, situated twelve miles to the south of Sun Valley. We drove through it on Sunday when we first arrived. While Ketchum accommodates the celebrities and wealthy guests with its shops full of beautiful, expensive, and totally unnecessary items, Hailey is where the local community procures practical items such as door hinges, green beans, and antifreeze.

2222

We drive the scenic route to Hailey, winding through the interior of the Wood River Valley. Bill, the organizer of this year's reunion, sits toward the front and uses the sound system in the bus to tell us interesting bits of information along the way.

"You see the house sitting up here on this hill to our left? That belongs to Clint Eastwood."

Bill, a stout man who stands more than six feet high, is probably in his early sixties and has a shock of bright white hair. He was an officer in the navy. Artis tells me that after his days in the service, Bill was a high school teacher. I would wager that he also coached something.

"And these houses over here," Bill says more, but my attention is drawn to the view through my window, a spectacular display of mustard yellow, pumpkin orange, fading green, and dusty brown vegetation growing in the valley. The snow tapers off as we travel further south into lower elevation, allowing us to see more of the autumn palette. It's not as if the fall colors in the Loess Hills are any less brilliant, it's just that I never tire of seeing them, no matter where I see them.

After about an hour, we arrive in Hailey, our stop for lunch. The microphone crackles as Bill makes another announcement.

"Now, we were gonna eat at a restaurant up in the Valley, but it's closed for the season. But this one is good, too."

Bill then gives us permission to go ashore.

While the group begins to file off, I duck in behind Mom and Dad to ask whether they want to go in or have me bring lunch to them.

"I'm gonna stay here," Dad says expectedly. "I don't wanna get on and off again. Bring me back a bowl of soup or somethin'."

"I'll bring you something back that you'll like," Mom volunteers. She's better than me when it comes to selecting food that will appeal to Dad.

We leave the bus and walk into a typical American diner serving milkshakes, burgers, and French fries. Bright red and yellow metal chairs surround similarly colored metal tables. Booths line the walls next to the windows, and a lunch counter with soda-jerk service anchors the center of the room.

We sit down with another couple, Frank and Susan from Illinois. Before we can learn more about our lunch companions, the waitress takes our order.

"I'm going to take this order out to the bus, so I need it to go," Mom directs the waitress. "But I want two hamburgers and two side orders of chili." She's not finished. "And two chocolate milkshakes."

I stare at her. Mom has no appetite at home, and Dad has no appetite on this trip. No way can they ever eat that much.

"I think your father would like that, don't you?" she asks me under the menu.

Our waitress is experienced and has obviously heard this order before.

"Actually, those are really big shakes," the woman wearing the apron explains. "I can get you two, but one is usually enough for two people."

Mom concedes one of the milkshakes, and when the chocolaty smooth ice cream arrives in two containers, she agrees she made the right choice. She carries the two tall glasses out to Dad on the bus while I wait at the table for the rest of our order.

The descent of fifty lunch patrons at one time taxes the wait and kitchen staff. Luckily, our table was first in line, and our food arrives before some have even had a chance to order.

"I'll be right back," I excuse myself to our new friends and take the extra larger burgers and steaming chili out to Mom and Dad.

Back on the bus, Dad has already become acquainted with Neil, the driver. In addition to his name, Dad has a general idea of where Neil's house is here in the Valley and has discovered why Neil chose this particular occupation. Dad's talents were wasted below deck in the navy. He should have worked in intelligence.

Neil parked the bus directly behind four cars, trapping them against the curb. Two annoyed drivers glare at the bus until Neil closes the door, moves the rectangle on wheels, and allows the cars to escape. Then he returns the bus to his original spot and resumes his visit with Dad.

"Why didn't Neil park somewhere else so he doesn't have to keep moving?" I whisper to Mom.

"Well, usually he finds an empty lot," Mom explains, "but he heard me say I was only going to be in the restaurant for a little bit, so he stayed put."

Only a few miles with my parents, and Neil already knew what would make life easier for both of them, even if it meant incurring the wrath of other drivers.

"Do you need anything else?" I ask my parents before returning to the restaurant.

"Nah," Dad replies. "We're good. We're gettin' to know Neil here."

Leaving them in capable and compassionate hands, I return to my own lunch and use the opportunity to learn more about why people attend these reunions.

"We actually had another one scheduled for this week, but I chose to come to this one," Frank tells me. He is a career serviceman who served on more than one ship.

"How many do you go to each year?" I ask him.

"Well, as many as I can. I feel a special kinship with the people. They're just a good group to be with." He describes his experiences at each reunion and how they compare with each other.

After finishing my lunch, I look around and realize that six tables are still waiting for their food. I excuse myself and return to the bus to see how Mom and Dad are passing the time.

"Did you see that quilt store as we drove in?" Mom asks me. "I think it's just around the corner."

Rather than asking him directly, we wait and watch Dad's face for a reaction to Mom's hint.

"You girls go right ahead," Dad says. "Neil's tellin' me about how this town got started."

In very little time, we find a small shop overflowing with patterns, threads, buttons, and bolts of cotton. Mom is particularly thrilled to discover a designer cloth for which she has been searching for months. A hand-tied fabric suitable for knitting catches my attention. We both leave the store satisfied with our purchases.

By the time we reboard, all of the other sailors and their spouses have finished lunch and are ready to tour the forest. Neil turns the bus north toward the Sawtooth Reserve, and Bill returns to the sound system to offer a history of the area.

"Sawtooth began as a national forest in 1905. Then the federal government set aside nearly 800,000 acres for protected recreational use. The area contains four mountain ranges with forty peaks above 10,000 feet and over 300 mountain lakes."

Today, thick gray clouds hang low over these peaks, making the mountains appear more formidable than inviting.

Artis changes seats to sit with me while Bud occupies both seats across the aisle. We have the entire afternoon to share.

"Show me what you bought," Artis says pointing at my bag.

I pull out the olive green print that has been sliced into strips and then tied together so it can be worked like yarn.

"I also enjoy knitting," she says. "It's so relaxing."

Unlike Artis, Mom doesn't knit. She sews. She sewed our prom dresses, nightgowns, and even some of our underwear. She made three or four beautiful dresses for Clare and Elisabeth when they were younger, but Mom's current interest is in machine embroidery.

I don't have the patience for sewing. In order for the garment to be a success, the cloth must be cut exactly like the pattern, the stitches can't be uneven from being dragged through the foot feed. Plus, one must understand and pay attention to something called a "bias." Whenever I sewed something, the reaction of my friends was always, "Did you make that yourself?"

Knitting doesn't require the same precision as sewing. Even a beginner can make a great-looking scarf.

"I like trying new yarns. I've even tried dying some yarn with Kool-Aid," I tell Artis.

"Oh, I have a niece who raises sheep and spins her own wool. I'll have to get you two together."

The conversation turns to more serious topics. Artis recounts her difficult divorce from her first husband and then tells me the agony of losing one of her children. Her daughter, a healthy young adult about to begin her career and life as a physician, died of an unexpected and rare medical condition. The loss nearly killed Artis as well.

"It shapes everything I see now, everything I do," she reflects. "It has brought me closer to God, or rather, to Mother Mary, knowing that Mary also experienced the loss of a child."

The road winds around the side of the mountain. If I were allowed to hold my hand out the window I could touch its cold walls. On the other side of the bus is sky, infinite and gray. No safety railing protects drivers from a careless mistake. One mistimed jerk of the wheel by Neil would send us all rolling like pumpkins down the mountain.

My religious convictions tend to wander dangerously close to the precipice on the other side of the road. Artis, though, has faith like my parents, a belief anchored securely next to the mountain wall. Rather than test her faith, her tragedies have only strengthened her confidence and belief in Christian theology.

Mom and Dad have had other friends with unshakeable faith. Paul Booten for example.

Paul Booten had no doubts regarding his Christian convictions. He also seemed to have an unusual affection for our family, particularly for his little "Ron-ae," as he called me. Each time we visited him, he repeated the story of how he held me when I was an infant.

"You were a-kickin' and a-laughin' and a-smilin' up at me, and I told your parents, there was somethin' special about you."

Paul owned a secondhand store in a tiny town about ten miles north of the farm. He sold a smorgasbord of used goods, from estate auction furniture to inventory damaged from trucking accidents. Paul bartered, traded, or pawned any item of any value. The shop spilled over with bicycles, wheels, car parts, milking machines, screws, bolts, and literally, kitchen sinks.

Always wearing a white shirt, long black tie, and black trousers, Paul's hair was shaved close, and his face was set off with thick black glasses.

The back portion of the store is where Paul lived with his wife, Joyce. A curtain divided the store from their simple apartment. Joyce's mental health was fragile. When customers shopped, she stayed behind the fabric wall, mumbling curses and warnings to Paul.

"They should leave now. People are just here to steal. They'll rob you blind. Take all your money."

Dad often took me with him to visit Paul's store, and Paul would try to draw his wife into the conversation.

"Joyce, Charles is here with Ron-ae. You remember Charles, don't you?"

"Of course I remember Charles," she spat back. "What, do you think, I'm from Norway or something?"

Paul allowed me to ride around the store on one of the tricycles for sale while Dad searched for a bolt or a gear. With Dad or any other customer, Paul never missed an opportunity to discuss the wages of sin, repentance, or other matters of eternal importance. His earnest demeanor probably cost him customers, but Paul would have considered the economic loss inconsequential.

Visits to Paul's store were less frequent once I began attending school. I didn't want to be around him as much anyway as I began to recognize how odd he really was. Despite my change in attitude toward Paul, he never abandoned his devotion to me.

"How is that little Ron-ae?" he always asked Dad, quickly inquiring about "the rest of the children, too," as an afterthought.

Long after I stopped visiting Paul entirely, my brother and I were wasting a typical summer afternoon taunting each other. What started off as simple teasing, though, ended in a high-speed chase around the front yard.

On the edge of our lawn grew a mature oak tree my Grandpa Charles had planted. The limbs climbed thirty feet or more into the air. Hooked from one of the lower branches dangled a long rope, the type used for pulling wagons or lifting bales of hay into the barn, and the kind that would tear hands raw if held too tight or climbed without gloves. With a short, flat board across the bottom loop of the rope, we could transform this farm tool into a great swing.

On the red Honda 90 typically used for farm chores, Rod pursued me as I rode my blue bicycle with the stingray handlebars. While speed was in his favor, I was clearly more agile. I evaded my brother with a hairpin turn around the back of the tall oak tree and aimed for the left side of the swing.

I made the turn but misjudged the swing. Still pedaling, the rope became a noose around my neck, jerking my body into the air while the bike continued forward. The fall against the hard-pack ground pounded all of the breath out of my lungs.

After the daze of the moment passed, I stood up to demonstrate to all that I had no broken bones. My only injury was a necklace burned around my throat but that would only last a week or two. Judging from Mom's expression as she watched all this transpire from the living room window, it was clear that I was in far better health than my brother was about to be.

Later that evening, we had an unexpected phone call from Paul Booten. He hurriedly asked Mom the obligatory social questions.

"How's the family?"

"We're all fine, Paul," Mom answered. "And how are you?"

"Well, I've just been a-sick to my stomach all day. I've been a-worryin'. Worryin' about little Ron-ae. All afternoon, I've been down on my knees a-prayin' for her, scared to death that somethin' terrible has happened."

I don't know what Mom said to Paul in their conversation. She never told me about his premonition until years after it happened. Hearing the story as an adult confuses me, but my inability to explain the event doesn't, in and of itself, transform the experience to a sacred level. It only complicates things.

"Maybe we can get the officers to buy us a beer at the next station," says one of the enlisted men in a deliberate attempt to stir up conversation and controversy in the bus. The men laugh.

"What do you think of these get-togethers, Artis?" I ask as we drive further down the road. "What is it that pulls these guys together?"

"Oh, you know, just the closeness of everyone," she tries to explain. "You see Sam up there?" She points to a man who is small in stature, but given the way others treat him, he clearly commands great respect from the other sailors.

"Well, several years ago, things were going bad for him. He and his wife divorced, and his daughter no longer spoke to him. He was using a lot of alcohol to keep it together. He wasn't doing well at all.

"Apparently, he was pretty much resolved to end his own life," Artis continues. "Someone convinced him to attend one of these reunions. I don't know what happened during that particular reunion, if something was said, or he had a realization, but as he tells it, he gained enough courage to face his problems and try again. He hasn't missed a reunion since."

I study the back of Sam's shoulders, wondering what he found.

"What about Bud? Why does he like to attend?"

"Well, for Bud, it's family," Artis says softly. "He's not close to his blood relatives, but he thinks of these men as his brothers. Like your own father, for example."

She hesitated long enough to look at Dad.

"Bud prays for Charles every single day."

I look away from Artis to see the splendor of the mountains. I look out the window so Artis won't see how her words have planted tears in my eyes.

"Ed wants to talk to your dad about his leg," Artis continues. Ed is a navy officer who regularly attends these reunions. Several years ago, he had his own arm amputated.

"He wants to tell your father about his own experience but doesn't want to speak out of turn. Do you think that would be all right?"

I often wonder myself about whether amputation of Dad's leg would save his life. If his doctors have offered it as an option, I'm not aware of it. Dad doesn't raise the issue, and neither do I.

"I don't know, Artis," I say sincerely.

Neil doesn't slow down much as we crest the mountain summit. He simply proceeds with the decent as if nothing significant has happened. The clouds clear a little when we stop at one of the small lakes to stretch and take photographs. We take another short break in Stanley, Idaho.

"Stanley is one of the coldest spots in the nation," Bill announces over the microphone. "Lots of records broken here."

I remain on the bus rather than experience any of its famous low temperatures.

Three of the officers patronize the small general store in Stanley and return with a six-pack of Moose Drool Beer to share with the others.

We're nearly home when the bus detours one last time to an overlook of the entire valley where we have spent the day exploring. I notice that Neil has again parked the bus at an awkward angle. Instead of between the lines as expected, he carelessly drove right across them, preventing any other cars, if there were any, from parking in these spaces.

The wind at the overlook is frosty, and over half of the group decide to stay inside. But those of us who can bear the cold wind are rewarded by a breathtaking vista. A wide swath of purple, green, and brown stretches out to the foothills and then melts into the mountains growing behind the vegetation. We can see for miles into the valley and imagine what animals might live in its embrace. I'm glad we made this stop.

Three sailors and their wives ask me to photograph them using the valley as a backdrop. The men seem to be feeling the effects of the Moose Drool Beer and probably don't really care about the quality of the picture. One of them even makes me a miniature snowman as thanks. When my fingers are too numb to press any more camera buttons, I board the bus and step in behind Mom and Dad. Dad has been in the same seat since eleven this morning and must be restless to return to the hotel.

He doesn't complain to me about his sore leg or cramped seat. Instead, he is distracted by what lies outside the bus window.

"Isn't that a sight?"

Casting my eyes to see what Dad sees, I realize that Neil didn't park randomly at all. Knowing Mom and Dad would not be able to leave their seats, he used particular care to position the bus in such a way to give them the best perspective of the valley.

Within the hour, Neil delivers us back to the resort. He helps us unload Dad, the wheelchair, and the walker. I think Mom left him a tip, but I add a little to the jar as well. I wish he had been our chauffer all the way from Omaha.

We use what is left of the setting sun to light our path back to the hotel room. With the aid of his walker, Dad welcomes the chance to move his legs. I roll the empty, folded wheelchair behind him. Walking feels good to me, too.

The idea of sitting through a long dinner tonight no longer appeals to me. Part of me regrets that Mom and Dad changed their minds about attending the barbeque.

Once we are back at the room, Dad lies down on the bed but leaves his shoes on his feet.

"What time we got to be up to the place, Ma?" he asks.

"Seven thirty. We have plenty of time for you to take a little nap. The boys said the place is just up the road here. Do you know how to get there, Rin?"

The bus actually drove past the location when we first left this morning. It's less than a mile away, on the same road as the hotel.

"I'm pretty sure I can find it."

Trail Creek Cabin is where we spend our evening. The rustic lodge is nestled into the side of the foothills along a mountain stream. Far enough away from the rest of the resort, it provides an intimate setting for private functions such as this one.

As we drive in, I search for the front door of the cabin, but the entrance faces the creek. The parking lot sits behind the restaurant.

"Go check it out, Rin," Dad instructs his scout.

I leave the heater blasting warm air on Dad, and Bud joins me in a mission to find an easy way for Dad to enter the cabin. To our dismay, four uneven steps lead down to the lodge landing. We survey the rest of the property, including the yard on the other side where Bill's son and his horse entertain the small group with cowboy tricks.

As Bud and I discuss whether Dad can manage the steps, we hear voices from behind the lodge.

"Just bring it around here!" The sailors call to us. "Bring the car across the lawn and pull up here."

Their suggestion would be an easier route for Dad because of the flat entrance, but the car will undoubtedly leave deep ruts in the grass if I drive over it. The navy buddies don't seem to be as concerned with the appearance of the lawn as they are about their friend. With their encouragement, I climb back inside the car, wipe the fog from the windows, and drive us directly behind the chairs of the other spectators. Dad has a great view of the show and stays comfortable inside the Buick where the temperature hovers around eighty.

After Bill's son demonstrates a number of impressive tricks with his horse and rope, we help Dad with his walker into the cabin for dinner. The front room is dark with thick black wood beams and plank walls. A pair of wooden snowshoes hangs above the lighted stone fireplace, adding to the 1937 ambience. A dining room decorated with blue-checked tablecloths is to the left. To our right, a buffet table overflows with barbeque chicken and pork, potato salad, green salad, corn bread, corn on the cob, and green beans. Staff dressed in cowboy shirts, boots, and bandanas stand behind the mountains of food, ready to serve us.

Dad leans into his walker beside me and instructs me as to which and how much of each delicacy to load on his plate. He doesn't eat thirty-two dollars worth of food, but he is happy to be there. I set his plate next to Mom's and return to the line for my own dinner.

We enjoy the evening with the others at our table, discussing the day's bus trip and the earlier entertainment. As we finish our blueberry cobbler, one of the men mentions the general state of affairs in today's military, a hot topic even for this crowd. I don't even attempt to participate in the conversation.

With our stomachs full and eyes heavy, we drive back to the hotel. I think of what a hard day this must have been for Dad, having to sit the entire time in a bus, car, or wheelchair, unable to move or change position and watching others explore, laugh, and play in the snow.

"I can't get over that view we saw today," Dad interrupts my feelings of pity for him. "I'm going to remember that for the rest of my life, whether that's tomorrow or years from now. That was just something. That was worth this whole trip."

Tuesday

October 4

Today, I return to the great outdoors for my daily walk. The thin and crisp mountain air cuts short my first few breaths. Frost covers any cars left under the stars last night. Even though it is October, lawn sprinklers continue to spray water onto the grass, freezing on the sidewalks and streets in the early morning.

A loud sound rumbles behind me, and I turn to see a bright yellow rectangle on wheels full of children. Black letters written across the sides spell out the name of the school district to which it belongs. I'm not expecting to see a school bus in this tourist area, and the sight of it reminds me that the world continues to spin even though we have lost contact for a few days.

Behind the streets of these vacant holiday homes is a short ski run known as Dollar Mountain. The hotel brochure mentions that it is as a good location for family skiing or tubing. Being from Iowa and from the farm, our family never put on a pair of skis but that didn't stop us from roaring down the snowy hills on a six-person toboggan or a wooden sled with its rudimentary steering mechanism.

In the same way that I remember my elementary school as having giant basketball hoops and bathroom stalls towering over me, I believe the snowstorms of my childhood to be more severe and dangerous than anything we experience today. My siblings and I missed days of school when the icy gravel roads were too slippery for the buses. Dad's tractor regularly pulled neighbors out of snow banks and even cleared drifts in the middle of the night for at least one friend to drive to the hospital.

Adults saw it as a nuisance, but we used the snow for endless hours of fun. Dad built us twelve-foot mountains of white through which we tunneled and engineered forts, complete with shelves for our frozen ammunition. When the snow turned icy, we lugged our well-used sleds with rusty metal runners to the highest point of the lane.

After we layered ourselves on top of one another, we sped down the frozen glass, past the barn and house, through the gate to the lower pasture, until we hit a snow bank or an Osage orange tree, whichever came first. If Dad finished his chores and saw us coming, he galloped alongside until he matched our speed and then flopped on top of us. Rather than give us additional momentum, though, his added weight usually stopped us completely.

When we could no longer feel our toes and fingers, we trampled inside and draped our wet clothes near the wood stove. On really good days, Mom warmed our insides with hot chocolate and donuts fresh from the frying pan, dripping with glaze.

The temperature must be around forty degrees this morning. I notice that Dollar Mountain wears no white this morning. When I reach Clint Eastwood's house, I reverse course and return to the hotel to eat breakfast with Mom and Dad in the room.

Dad is already at the glass table trying to stab open the single-serving box of Rice Crispies Mom bought in Mammoth Springs. His lower right leg is dark purple and bloated. In fact, nothing from his knee down appears healthy. By the time I finish my shower, he's under the blankets again, fully clothed.

"I'm just going to nap for a little bit," Dad says. "Why don't you girls go paint up the town or something?"

Knowing he will rest better if we aren't here, Mom wonders if I can find that Laundromat again.

"Sure," I say. "And there's a little yarn store I'd like to visit as well. You want us to bring you anything back, Dad?"

"No, you two just have a good time." His eyes are already closed. "Hey, turn that heat up a little before you go, will ya?"

I set the thermostat at eighty-two, and Mom covers him with more blankets.

"This isn't the way the bus came yesterday, is it?" Mom wonders when we are in the car headed into Ketchum.

On this trip, Dad has focused on his pain, and Mom has focused on Dad. Now that she has a break from being fully devoted to Dad's needs, Mom has trouble finding her role again, and, for some reason, her usually keen sense of direction.

"You're right, Mom. The bus didn't come this way. It went along a different side and made a loop. But I just want to drive directly into town."

"Oh, okay," she concedes.

Less than a minute passes before I hear, "I don't remember this road. Have we been on this one before?"

"Well, we came in on this road Sunday," I explain, "but we were going the opposite direction. Maybe it looks a little different."

Ketchum is only a mile or so away, and we quickly find both the town and the Laundromat.

I brought along one of my books to read while our clothes are spinning. As I sit down, however, my eyes are drawn to what sits on the table against the wall: a copy of the local telephone book. This resource, full of maps, ideas for recreation, safety information ("call before you dig"), and time zones, is a highly underappreciated cache of information.

After just a few minutes of opening the pages, I learn that Ketchum has expensive restaurants but that prospects for cheap pizza are further down the Valley. The book teaches me about the relatively high number of real estate agents working in the Valley, especially for a town of three thousand residents. I even analyze the surnames for clues as to national heritage.

Lessons in literature are in the phone book as well. Ketchum is home to the Ernest Hemingway Elementary School. In my forgotten lessons of history, I faintly connect Hemingway and Idaho, vaguely remembering that he spent some time in this town. I keep reading for more fascinating information.

Mom reads the biography I brought along, a more usual but far less interesting choice of reading material than what I study. The owner or manager of the Laundromat walks past Mom and me and then steps back to confirm what she sees. After staring for a few seconds, she makes the obvious statement.

"Are you readin' that phone book?" she asks incredulously. Then to no one in particular, "Here's one lady readin' a novel and the other readin' the phone book."

Mom must not have realized what I was doing because she casts a curious glance at what I hold in my hands. I shrug my shoulders in defense, abandon my book of valuable lists, and fish the warm clothes from the dryers. After carefully folding the shirts and pants, I toss assorted undergarments in the bag as quickly as I can, especially trying to avoid looking at items that don't belong to me.

After we leave the Laundromat, I make my mother an unwitting partner in the search for the knitting shop I hoped to visit. We find it situated in a cozy corner on the second floor of a small shopping area along the street. Shelves full of luxurious colors, textures, and weaves, including a number of locally produced yarn, overwhelm us the moment we step through the door. A deep brown mohair yarn would twin perfectly with the fabric strand I bought yesterday in Hailey. I justify my purchase with a plan to knit a scarf for Mom's birthday coming up in December.

With no other stores of particular interest to us, we amble aimlessly along the streets, peering through the windows, wondering who would wear what and to what function. We enjoy the ambience of the town without the deluge of tourists and walk together as friends without being confined to our traditional roles of mother and daughter.

When we pass a downtown grocery, scents from its delicatessen fill our noses and our imaginations. The inviting aroma leads us to three vats of soup simmering on a high table.

"I think your father would enjoy this for lunch," Mom says.

On a cold day like today, so would I. We ladle out a bowl each of chili, chicken-noodle, and mushroom soup, adding crackers and three large cookies to round out the meal.

The soups are still hot when we return to the hotel. Dad samples each one, but after tasting the mushroom soup, he says, "I like this one," and finishes it up.

One of the finest gifts an Iowa spring offers is a morel mushroom. Each May, my Grandma Bessie taught her grandchildren to scour the timber for cream-colored stems with ugly gray sponge tops. Dad hunted mushrooms with us as well, pointing out the dead elm trees where the succulent fungi supposedly flourished.

After our plastic bread sacks were brimming, we handed them over to Mom for a twenty-four-hour salt-water bath. A great deal of nature, living and dead, was released during these saline soakings, but I was too young to appreciate or understand the meaning of such details. As an adult, I join Dad each spring in anticipation of the smell and taste of a morel fried simply in butter and salt.

The mushrooms in this deli soup are definitely not morels, but at least they provide a flavor that wakens Dad's appetite. I'm glad we found something that finally appeals to him.

A ship auction is scheduled after lunch. Sailors and their spouses bring various items from home to sell. The proceeds from the sale pay for the mailings and any administrative costs of the reunions. Photographs are scheduled for five o'clock, and the farewell banquet begins at seven.

Numerous times in the Tetons and Yellowstone, I yearned to jump out of the car and walk some of the trails in the parks. A brochure in the Sun Valley room promotes Bald Mountain as a premium recreational spot, not only for skiing in the winter, but hiking in the summer. Located on the other side of Ketchum, the mountain peaks are slightly over 9,000 feet above sea level, 3,400 feet from top to bottom.

I'd rather be on that mountain than at the auction. "Would you guys be okay if I walked the trail to the top?" I'm not so much asking for permission as I am seeking confirmation that my parents will be able to get themselves to the auction this afternoon. Refreshed from his morning nap and afternoon soup, Dad seems strong enough to grip the wheels with his hands if Mom needs help moving the wheelchair to the Ram Room.

"Yes, yes," Dad assures me. "We'll be fine. It sounds like a great thing. But I wish you weren't going out alone."

"Don't worry. I'll take my cell phone," I say confidently, as if the technology could protect me from dangerous mountain conditions or wild beasts.

"Well, you be careful," Mom says. "Don't take any chances."

With a freedom I haven't felt in a week, I abandon my parents to the alumni of the *Passumpsic* and drive the LeSabre to a giant asphalt parking lot next to the trailhead. Given the number of white lines, thousands of cars must pack in this space during peak skiing season, but today I share the space with only two others.

A sign directs me to the Bald Mountain Trail and outlines the four-and-a-half-mile route to the top. According to the map, it takes two to three hours to ascend and an hour and half to climb down. It's one o'clock now. I'm no athlete, but I regularly walk three or four miles a day. Even with the steep grade, I'm reasonably confident I can be off the mountain long before the sun starts to set at five.

Bright sunshine floods the cloudless sky. The temperature hovers around sixty-five degrees Fahrenheit, ideal hiking weather. My brown leather purse contorts into a backpack with the mere adjustment of two straps. Packed inside are my fully charged bodyguard cell phone, a water bottle, and a camera. My light blue alpaca gloves and navy blue ear band are tucked in my jacket pockets in case it turns chilly on top.

I mark off the first steps with a strong, brisk stride. The first part of the trail is moderate and easy to navigate, although definitely an incline. The path cuts through a heavily forested area that allows only minimal sunlight through its branches. When I look ahead, I see how this single-width dirt trail decorates the side of the mountain like garland wrapping a Christmas tree.

Close to the two-mile mark, the forest opens up into a wide meadow. The grass is tall and dry, but wild flowers still bloom, reminding me of a set from *The Sound of Music*.

A wood structure sits slightly off the track. On closer investigation, I discover it's an overlook tower with an expansive view of the town and southern valley. The horizon extends for miles, and the cars on the highway are nothing more than moving dots. I snap a photograph to show Mom and Dad later.

The path leads back into the trees. Even though I can't see it, I assume the summit sits on the other side of the hill. No other people or critters join me as I walk, although I do see fresh tracks. Researching what animals live on this mountain might have been smart preparation before trespassing through their habitat.

Now the trail slips in and out of the trees so that I move from sunlight to shade and back again frequently. Out in the open, the sun's rays are warm, and I only reluctantly return to the path underneath the trees. I pay less attention to the scenery now and concentrate instead on finding the path partially hidden by the snow.

Finally, I see the marker for three miles. Feeling the chill of the higher altitude, I stop to pull on my gloves and headband. I also zip up my coat tightly against my neck. The hike has been enjoyable, but I am tired now and grateful that I'm over halfway to the top.

As I set out again, I step into snow three inches deep, even more in the open field. This makes my shoes wet and my toes numb.

I should have brought mittens instead of these thin gloves. Even my knuckles ache when I force them to bend.

According to the signs along the trail, a water fountain is just ahead. I still have water in my bottle, but I'm saving that for when I reach the top. With the fountain at last in sight, I look forward to a long, refreshing quench of my thirst. The handle turns easily, but nothing splashes out. No water. Not even a drip. The main pipe obviously has been disconnected for the season. I satisfy myself with a quick swallow from my plastic bottle and dream of being back in the hotel, snuggling between the blankets reading one of my books or knitting something soft.

The clouds have turned to thick gray putty, nothing resembling the clear sky I saw in Ketchum that lured me to the mountain. Flurries begin to fall on my face, and unlike the snowflakes we saw in Yellowstone, these are small and dense.

I hesitate to double back because less than two miles remain to the top. I am sure to reach the summit in less time that it would take to return on the same trail. Besides, a smidgen of blue nudges through the clouds and convinces me it's wiser to press on to the top and return via the service road.

Often the trail crosses the ski runs. Because most of my effort is zigzagging the mountain, it would be considerably faster to climb directly up the hill, grabbing the tall grass to help pull me up the incline. It takes only a few steps for me to realize that I know nothing about mountains. This incline is far too steep to climb, and I'm forced to stay on the trail and take the long way to the top.

Each time I think I see the summit, I'm disappointedly wrong. The trail continues to wind around the mountain. Maybe no mountaintop actually exists. After all, we never found Grassy Lake. Instead of walking now, my feet are stomping along the trail because my toes won't bend. My fingers are inflexible as well.

"Don't take any chances." The words of my mother echo pointedly.

Ready to admit defeat, I search for the easy way to the top, the service road. I've crossed it numerous times in the past three miles, but now it's nowhere in sight. The only way to find the road used by utility vehicles is to keep climbing to the top of the mountain.

I am freezing and my feet and fingers are rigid. Every step is painful, and I feel foolish for underestimating the challenge of the mountain and overestimating my abilities to climb it. Like childbirth, if quitting close to the end were an option, I would choose it.

After three hours, I finally step onto the summit.

I had expected a feeling of satisfaction, accomplishment, something rewarding about reaching the pinnacle. Instead, all I feel is cold, very cold, on this quiet and still mountain. I normally enjoy solitude but up here today, I feel very alone. The Lookout Restaurant, open for business during skiing season, is closed tight. The chairlifts are abandoned, frozen along the huge cables extending all the way down the mountainside.

I also expected a geographic peak of some sort. The top of this mountain is graded, ideal for vehicles, skiers, and group assembly. I step to the edge of the mountain, hoping to look down on a valley similar to what we saw yesterday. Because of the mountain's shape, the precipice prevents even a decent view of the landscape below. I don't even bother taking the camera out for a photograph.

My mountaintop experience, something I've anticipated all afternoon, is anticlimactic, even disappointing. I suppose the cold and tiredness of my body are partly to blame.

Then a kind of sadness overwhelms me, a sorrow that pains me more than my physical discomfort. I want to be home. I don't mean the fancy room in Sun Valley or even the farm in Iowa, but back in Des Moines where my family is enjoying record warm temperatures, where they sleep through the night, move in and out of the car in less than sixty seconds, and eat crispy fruits and vegetables three times a day. I want to return to roads I can navigate without looking at a map. I want to be with my friends who share my political views and don't criticize my choice of reading material.

Most of all, I want to be in a place where I do not have to see my father dying of cancer every single minute of every single day.

I cover my eyes and cheeks with my blue-gloved hands and take a very long, very deep breath. No one sees me on this mountaintop. No one will rescue me or my father.

It's four o'clock and the sun has already started its descent on the other side of the mountain. The sign at the trailhead estimated an hour and a half to return. I drain my water bottle knowing that I'll soon have access to more. As I give a final looking around the mountain plateau, I see nothing that remains for me to explore. Using the dirt service road, I start downhill.

My legs are a little shaky, but I start to jog slowly down the mountain. I forget this isn't simply a hill. This is a ski slope where steep gradient is highly valued. Additionally, the road is muddy from the earlier snow. Without warning, I lose my footing and nearly trip over my feet. While this would be a faster way to the bottom, I don't want to be a human pumpkin today. I throw out my arms and regain my balance. Obviously, downhill running isn't an option for me.

After about fifteen minutes, three crewmen in a truck pass me on their way up the mountain. First, I wonder where they are going because I didn't see anything on the top that needed repaired. My second thought was how the truck managed to maintain all four wheels on the ground instead of flipping backwards over itself. Not wanting to appear as a crazy woman insufficiently dressed for a mountain hike, I fumble with my transformer purse and find my camera. I force my fingers to click the button twice to make it appear to the truck riders that I had deliberately planned this photo opportunity.

Actually, the photo shoot gives me a grateful excuse to rest my angry knees. They didn't hurt on the way up, but this downward slope is stretching muscles and ligaments that had no life before today. When the truck is out of sight, I continue down the mountain—backwards.

The pain is excruciating. While Dad's agony grows behind his joint, my pain sears in front of my knees. If what I feel is even a portion of what he experiences daily, then Dad's moaning, snipping, and attempts to protect his leg are instantly understandable. My appreciation for his circumstances grows with each stride.

"Count the steps," I coach myself down the hill. "Walk backwards twenty-five steps. Then turn around and walk ten."

The pain is sharp, stabbing, and unrelenting. More coaxing.

"I can do this. I'm almost there. This is the easy part."

I pass a couple with a dog, and then several more humans appear on the road.

"They're taking the easy way to the top," I grumble under my breath, angry for not thinking of it myself.

Eventually, I see the equipment buildings next to the lift house, then the lodge and gift shop. By 5:30 p.m., I walk off the grassy slope onto the flat paving bricks at the entrance to the ski area.

A huge sigh leaves my lungs as I open the door to the LeSabre. I use the same techniques Dad has modeled on this trip to contort my body into the car. Unable to grip the steering wheel because of frozen-finger syndrome, I simply rest my hands flat on the front of the edges. And also like Dad, as soon as I turn over the engine, I push the heat switch to the far red end and blast the air against my feet and face.

Mom and Dad left a note on the glass table that they are already at the reception. I still need to clean and warm up before I join them. With water as hot as I can stand, I sink into the deep white bathtub, absorbing heat into every pore. At first it stings my fingers and toes. My thighs and stomach are scarlet from the cold, and I shiver from my neck to my feet. After fifteen minutes, I relax and begin to feel warm again.

Still basking in the hot water, I hear the door unlock.

"Are you here, Rin?" Mom has come to find me.

"In the bathroom. Sorry I didn't call you to let you know I was back."

Mom wasn't really worried. Mostly she wanted an excuse to break away from the group. She enjoys their company, but like me, she covets time alone.

I snuggle inside one of the hotel's plush robes. If Mom hadn't returned to the room, I would have flopped down on the bed and fallen into a deep sleep. But my moment of exploration is over now, and I'm expected to attend the reunion's final social event.

My khaki pants and sweater look very plain, even frumpy, when I stand next to Mom. She's wearing a classic black dress topped with a bright fuchsia jacket. A pair of black round earrings completes the outfit. To those waiting for us in the banquet room, she will appear confident and calm. No one will suspect how the burden of Dad's cancer, the anticipation of loss as well as the details of his daily care, weighs on her shoulders.

When Mom and I return to the banquet room, Dad has already wheeled his chair up to a round table set for eight. He hasn't used his walker much today, feeling more comfortable in the wheelchair. Mom sits to his left, and Artis and Bud are on the other side of him. Everyone at the table, including me, wears a nametag.

"Hello, Gloria. Where have you been all day?"

"I climbed to the top of Bald Mountain," I answer with confidence now that I have returned. I may have answered differently three hours ago.

"Did you have a good walk, Rin?" Dad asks with a tired voice. A maroon knit vest fits around him snugly. His plaid blue shirt beneath is not quite buttoned to the top, and his white T-shirt shows through. His face is flushed again, with eyes barely able to stay open.

He makes a nondescript general motion toward Mom, signaling her in a way that only a partner of fifty years can understand. Without hesitation, she draws pain medication from her purse and slips it to him as stealthily as a magician hiding a secret trick.

"It was great," I say, which is mostly true. Pride prevents me from fully admitting careless preparation on my part. "I started to get a little cold, though."

Dad closes his eyes and rests his forehead in his right hand. He may be listening, but I address the rest of the Bald Mountain details to Bud until the official ceremony begins.

"I want to thank everyone for being here tonight," Bill welcomes us from the lectern. "This is a very special group, and I am honored to be with you."

Our host recounts a story of a fellow serviceman who served on the *Passumpsic* with him during the Vietnam War. The other sailor apparently volunteered for a transfer to another ship only to be killed soon after he left. Bill is haunted by the memory of this man, knowing that it could have been Bill who volunteered for the transfer instead.

The retired sailors then commemorate a solemn, even sacred tradition, the two-bell ceremony. At the end of each sea day on the *Passumpsic*, a bell was rung twice, followed by the playing of Taps. In the ceremony tonight, one man reads the names of the shipmates who died throughout the year, while another rings a humble, unpolished brass bell two times for each name. The somber timbre echoes through the room. Two or three in the room look directly at the man reading the names or the one ringing the bell. Others stare at the floor.

Next year, they will ring the bell for my father.

After our banquet dishes are cleared, Bill issues an open invitation.

"I'd like to open this up to anyone who would like to address the group. I had my chance earlier and maybe the rest of you would like to say something."

Unsurprisingly, patriotism and honor are the major themes that resonate with this group.

"America is the greatest nation in the world," the first person stands to say. "And the reason America is so great is because it is a Christian nation. If we lose sight of that, we will no longer be great."

He receives confirmation of his beliefs from most of the people in the room. After a few more people speak on the same topic, I see Sam, the man Artis described to me on the bus, approach the microphone. He wears his original navy uniform, and I am amazed at how well it still fits him.

"I love this country," he says passionately. "I am proud to be an American. But we are at war right now, and we can't tolerate anybody tearing down this country. I'd like to kick out of this country every card-carrying member of the ACLU right now."

Loud cheers erupt, accompanied by robust applause.

Next, a woman younger than me stands to add her voice. Her father was a sailor on the *Passumpsic* about the same time frame as Dad, although I don't think they ever served on the same tour. Her father died three years ago, but she and her mother wanted to attend this reunion even in his absence.

"I'm not important enough to stand up there as you all are doing," she says, "so I'm just gonna say what I have to say down here." She proceeds to use a hand-held microphone rather than the one attached to the lectern.

"I teach grade school, and I'm sick of people telling me that my kids can't pray and that I can't talk about God in the classroom. But I want you to know that I don't care what 'they' say. I'm gonna keep on teachin' God 'n' country in my classroom until God tells me to quit."

More clapping.

At first, personal feelings of disagreement grow inside of me through all of these speeches. I long to demonstrate the freedom of speech concept by voicing an alternative view. Then I look across the table and see Dad's slumping shoulders and closed eyes. He most likely agrees with everything his friends say, but I don't believe his focus is on their words right now. Likewise, when I see my father so resigned, my instincts to care about America, Christianity, or the ACLU suddenly melt away.

No one else adds to the forum, and discussion ensues about the location of the next two reunions. Volunteers are needed to host and organize the weekend. The group is also mindful to alternate the geographical location each year in order that more are able to participate. When the plans are sufficiently outlined for next year, Bill returns to the microphone to close the reunion.

"It is difficult to explain to others the bond that is created between men who serve in a common cause together. We covered each other's back, laughed with each other, and may have even fought amongst ourselves. And even though we may have served at different times and didn't meet each other until this weekend, we are truly brothers.

"Now before we leave tonight, one of us here needs a lot of prayers and God's healing touch. Charles, if you'll let us, I want you to come up here and sit. And those of you who want to join us, come up here, too, and place your hands on Charles while I say a prayer on his behalf."

I look to Mom and Dad to see if they are either surprised or uncomfortable, but they don't seem affected. Slowly, deliberately, but without hesitation, Dad lifts himself out of his wheelchair and uses his walker to move to the front of the room. When he reaches the waiting metal folding chair, he falls hard into the seat.

As Bill begins his prayer for healing, the men surrounding the chair extend their arms to touch my father's shoulders, arms, back, and head. Dad's face glows from the fever but reveals nothing of what he feels.

The prayer is short, and the men help Dad to his feet. Bud walks beside Dad back to the table and helps him into his wheelchair.

"All right, Sailors," Bill addresses the group for the final time. "This reunion is officially closed."

Applause fills the room. I stand and stretch before walking around the table to help Dad start rolling in the direction of the door.

"Dad, do you want to stay to talk to some more people?" I see others moving around the room, saying their farewells until next year.

"Nah. I had a good talk with them all this afternoon. Let's get back to the room." His throbbing leg hides beneath his trousers.

Dad shakes hands with Bud on his way out.

"I'll see you guys back in Council Bluffs," Dad tells his friend. "You've got a lot of driving ahead of you."

"Good-bye, Gloria," Bud says.

Mom walks beside me as I push Dad to the exit. Friends block our path to wish us luck and promise to pray for Dad. Just as we are about to break for the tall wooden doors, I sense someone moving quickly along our right side. Rather than another graying sailor, this time it is the bartender who steps into our path. As he stands directly in front of Dad, I recognize him as the same person who produced the wheelchair when we first arrived and the one who made the adjustments to the wheelchair footplates. With great tenderness and respect, he bends over and grasps Dad's hand.

"Sir, I just want to thank you for your service to our country." He pauses and then hesitates, unsure how to phrase his next words.

"And sir, I really hope you feel better."

The words of this man, someone we just met, and someone we will never see again, surprise and humble me. I don't know how to respond but Dad does.

"Well, thank you, son," my father replies sincerely and quietly. "It was nice gettin' to know you, too."

We leave the banquet room without any other interruptions.

Wednesday

October 5

Last night, Mom put an ice pack on Dad's shin to reduce the swelling, but he didn't even know it was there. Today, we're having trouble fitting his foot into his shoe. We unloosen the laces until they nearly fall out, allowing his right foot to slip in far enough to give him some protection. As gently as she can, Mom starts to tie his shoe more securely.

"Carn sound-it, woman." Dad uses more of his unique vernacular. "Can't you do that a little more softly?"

We're in for a long trip back to Salt Lake City. And not just Dad. When I woke up this morning, my knees and shins ached, as did other parts of my legs that I didn't know existed. Instead of sliding my legs out of bed and standing upright, I sort of rolled over, up, and out all at the same time, minimizing any sharp and halting movements.

After we shower and dress, Mom and I pack our dirty clothes away in used plastic shopping sacks before placing them with the rest of the luggage. I load the car and move it to the nearest spot in the parking lot. Dad takes a last-minute rest, and Mom checks the room for items we have forgotten to pack.

When Dad is ready, I return the wheelchair and our keys to the front desk. Dad uses the exit door next to our room and actually manages the two outside steps fairly easily. He quickly finds his three-step cadence and enjoys the walk, knowing he will be stuck in the car for the next five hours to Salt Lake City.

As we leave town, I point out Old Baldy to show Mom and Dad where I spent my yesterday afternoon.

"I wish I could have been up there with you, Rin," Dad says.

"Yeah. Lots of spots would have made good test runs for our pumpkins." I don't mention my burning knees.

"Well, good for you for doin' that."

He's glad I had the opportunity to climb a hill. I hope that he is also proud that I made the trek, for adventuring to a place he would have gone as well, if he could walk.

My thoughts catch me by surprise. If I were to ask my parents right now, out loud in this car, whether they are proud of me, I know how they would answer. It would be the same answer I would give my children.

"Of course, we're proud of you. We love you. Why are you even asking?"

At this point in my life, it's silly that I still care whether my parents are proud of me. My feelings seem like those of a kindergartener bringing home a Crayola drawing, hoping Mom and Dad will hang it on the refrigerator door.

I suddenly realize that my selections of mountain roads, soft meals, and evening accommodations were only my attempts to please my parents, maybe even impress them. They couldn't care less where we drove, what we ate, or where we slept. They never asked for any of these things. They never even asked me to be here. Clearly, I didn't make this trip for Mom and Dad. I made this trip for me.

No matter how many miles we drive or bears we don't see, they will still love me the same when we return to Iowa as they did before we left. Apparently, I will never outgrow my need for their unconditional love and approval.

Perhaps the feeling runs in the family. After Dad finished his service with the navy, he and Mom married. While Mom taught school, Dad, who had already passed his GED, used the GI Bill to attend college where he received an associate of arts degree. His education opened up another world to Dad, the world of history, science, and literature.

Dad returned to the farm after college but continued to kindle a desire to teach high school history. He and Mom talked about the idea with each other and even prayed about it. Finally, they agreed Dad should return to college for a teaching certificate.

My parents understood that their plan would not only affect them, but also my grandparents. Dad would no longer be around to help Grandpa, already in his late seventies, with the farm. He might not even find a teaching position in Iowa. Dad summoned all the courage he could muster before he broached the subject with his parents.

According to Mom, the teaching idea was not well received. Dad helped to provide an income for my grandparents. Perhaps Grandma and Grandpa couldn't bear to lose their youngest son even to geography.

I don't know how the discussion ended, but Dad never became a teacher. He stayed on the farm the rest of his life; a decision that both he and Mom knew pleased his parents.

A rest area halfway between Sun Valley and Salt Lake City provides us with a break in our miles. My muscles didn't hurt while I was driving, so I am surprised how quickly my legs turn to rubber when I step out of the car to stretch. I catch myself against the door before either Mom or Dad sees anything. If Dad knew about the sharp stabbing pains attacking my knees, he would demand to drive the rest of the way.

"How ya' feel today, Rin, after that big ol' hike yesterday?" Dad asks. Suspicious of his question, I answer cautiously.

"A little sore, but I'm okay." I sneak two Tylenol from my purse. "I'll be right back." I want to walk out some knots in my thigh muscles.

Our break is a short but sufficient one. Dad uses the bathroom, grateful for the chance to stretch. We quickly return to the interstate and see the Utah state line ahead. One last time before we cross the border we admire Idaho's expansive and extravagant landscape. The mountains are undeniably a stark contrast to the rolling hills of Iowa, but we found enough similarities in the state's farm country to form a bond with its beauty. The colors and textures of the peaks and valleys are forever etched in our memories, even if we never again return to these majestic sites.

"How many different license plates did we get, Mom?" I call back to her for some conversation. She tallies up the names of the states listed on the yellow legal pad of paper.

"I think we have thirty-eight and two from Canada. Once we left Yellowstone, we really didn't see many others."

"Bummer," Dad says just before he drifts off to sleep again. Mom quickly follows him in slumber.

I'm tired from my walk yesterday, but Mom and Dad are exhausted from their relentless battle with Dad's cancer. Mom guards Dad's right limb and waits on his every need. Dad is frustrated that he has to move at a snail's pace with his walker, doubting even his sense of balance.

This week has also been difficult emotionally. It has been heartbreaking for me to see Dad lose interest in most all conversation and activity. I've always seen my father persevere, to overcome events and circumstances that were beyond his control.

The spring of 1985 particularly tested his limits. By this time, Grandma Bessie was widowed, and Dad checked on his mother daily. She welcomed her baby boy with cherry pie, cookies, or other freshly baked items. Always active, alert, and independent, Grandma surprised us all when her heart gave out so quickly.

About two months earlier, Dad had purchased a new breed of beef cattle at a local sale barn. After several calves aborted, a visit from the veterinarian confirmed that the entire herd was infected with brucellosis and required quarantine. The cows must have been infected with the virus even before he brought them home. Health inspectors continued to monitor the cattle for months, but each time at least one of them tested positive for the disease. Dad received a letter from the government advising him that his entire herd had to be destroyed the exact same day he buried his mother.

With the sting of his mother's death and the slaughter of the cows still hanging over him, Dad suffered a third blow, the loss of a very old Jack Russell mutt named Spike. Dad and his dog were inseparable. Spike napped next to Dad during the day and ate scraps of food Dad fed him under the table when Mom wasn't looking. When Dad checked the fence, Spike ran beside him. If Dad drove the truck to the windmill, Spike rode with him. When Dad called him Tough Man and teased him, Spike growled back and asked for more. Spike even forgave Dad for running him over with a tractor, allowing Dad to nurse him back to health.

On a night soon after Grandma had died, Dad finished watching the ten o'clock news and opened the front door for Spike to go outside, the same as they had done every other night. When Dad called his dog back, Spike didn't show. Dad searched through the barns, the apple orchard, and even by the creek, but his small, white and brown-spotted companion never returned.

Dad faces his cancer today the same way he faced the heartache that spring, pragmatically but unwilling to accept defeat. Soon after Dad received his terminal diagnosis, we convened a family meeting to learn how Dad wanted us to run the farm, what needed to be done to keep it intact, and anything else he wanted to share with us.

"It's not a done deal," Dad said, refusing to believe he was powerless over the cancer. "I'm not giving up. I intend to beat this thing."

His farming advice was vague and only repeated the obvious: keep the fence mended, the tractors in good repair, and the house painted. He saw no purpose in detailed instructions if he would be present to dole out dribbles of information himself.

My eyes are on the road ahead, but I am fully aware of the stranger who sleeps in the seat next to me, pale and restless. I wonder how long he can defend against the revolution assaulting his body. How tempting it would be for Dad to lie down on the living room sofa, fold his arms across his chest, and sleep forever in the heat of the wood fire.

We arrive back in Salt Lake with ample time before our flight is scheduled for departure. The same English-accented Alamo clerk we met last week recognizes us and remembers Dad's limitations. Graciously, after we turn in our keys, she drives us directly to our terminal to save us the walk.

Outside of the airport doors, we wave down a skycap, a twenty-year-old woman with the name Jenny on her uniform. Dad accepts the wheelchair she offers, folding his walker and laying it across the arm rests.

Just as we did in Omaha, Mom and I walk through security on one side while Dad pulls himself upright and is subjected to a private scan. After clearing security, Jenny leads us to our gate, the one at the farthest end of the airport.

Jenny is, without a doubt, the best skycap we have had on this trip. The other skycaps rushed Dad down the ramps, frightening him with the possibility of being tossed headfirst from the chair at any moment. Instead, Jenny spins the wheelchair around at each down ramp and walks backwards. In this way, she stays in total control of the speed and slope. She also slows for each seam and change in the flooring, minimizing rather than emphasizing the bumps. Dad is much more relaxed with her than he has been with any other chair driver, including his daughter.

"Who's got my walker?"

Mom's eyes meet mine in panic. We look at Jenny who has a grip on dad's chair. We desperately hope it's dangling from the handlebars. Jenny only stares blankly back at us.

Stupid walker. I must have left it at the end of the x-ray machine.

"You go on to the gate," I say as if it's no big deal. "I'll go back to the security area and find it."

Ignoring the loud protest from my knees, I retrace my steps past the previous twenty-four gates as quickly as I can. Even the escalator is too slow. I gallop down the stairs instead.

"Please let it be there. Please let it be there," I repeat over in my head knowing exactly what it means if I have lost the one piece of equipment Dad truly requires and entrusted to my care. At least his name and address are emblazoned upon it. If security has confiscated the walker, they'll know where to return it.

As I approach the security thresholds, a wave of relief flows over me. The stainless steel contraption sits camouflaged next to the silver trays catching the carry-on bags after x-ray. No one questions or even notices me as I snatch it from its hiding place.

I hurry back to Mom and Dad, crossing Jenny's path as she pushes her wheelchair to meet another passenger.

"May I have your attention, please, ladies and gentlemen," booms a voice over the intercom. I join Mom and Dad at our gate. "All traffic in and out of Las Vegas is delayed on account of the high winds in Nevada."

Las Vegas is where we will meet our connection to Omaha. Dad moves so slowly that I worry we won't have enough time to change gates at the airport if our flight from Salt Lake City is delayed. I really don't want to miss that flight to Omaha. Overnighting in Las Vegas with my parents is not a comforting thought.

As more flights are delayed, the terminal crowds with people. Every chair at the gate is filled. Dad grows nervous and finds new ways to protect his sore leg.

Fortunately, my worry is for naught. Either the winds cleared or the crisis otherwise passed. Within an hour of our scheduled departure time, we leave the mountains of Utah beneath us and make up time in the air.

After this flight, we only have one more leg to Omaha. Once we board that plane, my responsibilities to my parents will be all but over.

I recently heard a radio news report that the most dangerous time for soldiers in a war zone is immediately after arrival and just prior to returning home. According to the experts, soldiers let their guard down and are most careless during these times.

We land in Nevada, and the wartime phenomenon strikes. Two wheelchairs wait at the gate but only one skycap. Another passenger from our flight needs to make a connection sooner than our own. I offer to push Dad to our gate myself, and the problem is easily solved. Or so I think.

Mom is once again skeptical of my navigation skills.

"Is this the right direction?" she asks.

I point to the signs that direct us to our gate. Dad keeps a tight grip on his walker lying across his lap, not letting it out of his sight again.

"What is the number?" she demands.

"C25," I repeat, this time showing her our boarding passes.

"Wheel! Of! Fortune!" screams at us from across the terminal. The constant techno-whirling from the slot machines is more than annoying. Background music, designed to tame the edgy traveler, only adds to our confusion. As if that is not enough, a continuous bombardment of announcements warns passengers not to leave bags unattended or to smoke inside the terminal.

The repetitive assaults of noises and lights discombobulate Mom. Dad's hearing, already compromised by years of listening to the roar of his tractors, corn dryers, and grain augers, cannot discern the separate sounds under these conditions. Instead, he shuts himself off and leaves the task of finding the correct gate to Mom and me.

"We have gone too far," Mom practically shouts just as I stop directly in front of the C25 sign.

"I'll go get our blue preboarding passes," I say, wanting to escape from them both.

Before I approach the ticket counter, only twenty feet away, I park Dad out of the path of other passengers and pull up the brake on his chair. I take only five steps before Dad's cry fills the terminal, a sound I have feared the entire trip.

"Ah, ah, ah!" Dad yelps. I jerk around to see what is left of a short businessman tripping over the wheelchair, bumping directly into Dad's right leg.

"I'm sorry. I'm so sorry." The traveler begs forgiveness with a slightly bewildered look. He realizes he has caused great pain to this old man but also knows the contact with Dad was nothing more than a brush. I abandon the boarding pass line and dash back to Dad.

"It'll be okay. It's okay." I encourage the stranger to move away from Dad as fast as possible. Dad calms down, but now he views each traveler in the terminal as a genuine threat to his leg.

"Do you want to walk it off a little, Dad?" I hope that a change in position will help dissolve the sting. After so much sitting today, he needs to stand as much as possible. He agrees, and I help him upright.

"You need to go with him," Mom commands, not because she blames me, but because she wants no further incident. "Make sure he is okay."

Not wanting to disobey my mother but not wanting to embarrass Dad, I follow at a discreet distance. He goes into the bathroom, and I take a long drink at the adjacent water fountain. When I turn around, the expression on Mom's face has moved from apprehension to outright worry. I risk going back to where she is standing, certain that Dad will not be out any time soon.

"They called our flight." Her tone reflects her concern.

"Are you sure?" I try to sound unflustered. "It's not time yet."

"Yes, they called our gate and our flight number."

So close to home. So close to the end of my shift. "Hey, weren't we supposed to call Rhonda?" I attempt to distract Mom. Last night, Rhonda called us at the hotel to confirm our flight details and asked that we phone when we were en route in case of any changes or delays in the travel plans.

"This would be a good time to call her and let her know everything is on track."

"There isn't time. We need to get on the plane."

Dad is still in the bathroom, but she is ready to go after him.

"Do you want me to go check at the desk about the flight?" I ask her. "Or let's go check the departures on the screen."

We walk over to the wall of television monitors flashing arrivals and departure schedules.

"See?" Her finger underlines one of the departing flights from our gate. "This is our flight. The man on the speaker said 'Omaha.' We need to get in line to board."

Mom has read the flight information for a flight originating in Omaha and continuing on to Los Angeles. Coincidentally, that flight is boarding now. Our flight, on the other hand, travels the exact reverse route, originating in LA and stopping in Las Vegas before flying into Omaha. The stopover cities are the same but the itineraries are assigned different flight numbers.

I understand Mom's confusion, but despite my attempts, I cannot diffuse her angst.

"We need to be on that plane," she insists.

I glance over at the bathrooms, but Dad doesn't appear. I show Mom the different arrival and departure screens again, pointing out the two different flights.

"This is our flight here, and it isn't leaving yet." I get confused by it all myself, sometimes.

"Okay," she seems satisfied for the moment. "I was looking at the wrong screen."

Dad emerges from the bathroom. As if waiting for the right opportunity, Mom springs in his direction.

"You need to get into the wheelchair right away so we can board."

I stare at her in amazement.

"We aren't boarding yet, are we?" Dad looks at me directly for verification. If I say no, Mom will look foolish, and then she will be even angrier with me. But this is not our flight. I don't want Dad to sit in that wheelchair until he absolutely must.

"No, not yet," I answer quietly. Mom looks betrayed.

"Sit in the chair anyway," Mom directs, "so that we are ready when we do have to board."

Dad starts to sit but Mom's leg catches between him and the chair. She falls into his lap.

"Well, move then," Dad snarls at her.

"You need to let me get out of the way first," she returns fire.

Each of us have held ourselves together fairly well on this trip, respectful of the feelings of our fellow travelers before giving a response. Now, like the soldiers about to return home, our guard is down, and we find ourselves in a Las Vegas minefield.

"I'm going to call Rhonda and let her know that we're going to be on time," I say and then find an empty chair away from the gate.

Using my cell phone, I update Rhonda about the trip in general and the last episode, specifically. She sympathizes and assures me she will be waiting at the airport for us.

Finally, our flight is announced, and we leave the dangerous air terminal behind. Unlike our flights west, Dad now wants to sit next to the window. He edges his way inside, safe from any clumsy passengers. Mom settles in the middle seat. I guard my parents from any aisle intrusions.

Once the plane lifts off, both parents fall asleep. I finish reading my second book of the trip and then stash it away in my carry-on bag, careful not to disturb my softly snoring mother.

The plane heads due east, which dims the cabin more quickly than our clocks suggest. My own reading light is off now, but I'm not sleepy. I relax in the darkness both inside the cabin and over the wings. Even the sound from the plane's engine shields me from unwanted distractions or stray conversations.

Mom is still asleep, but beyond her silhouette I notice Dad stirring, peering through the small oval window into the black heavens. His eyes are filled with the sadness that comes from knowing this is the last flight he will ever take. His face reflects both reluctance and resignation as he gazes between the darkness outside the plane and his fingers laced together on his lap.

I look down at my own hands and notice the two pieces of jewelry I always wear. My left hand bears my wedding band, dented and dull. The ridge around the beaded edge is worn down and is nearly smooth. I've long stopped wearing my engagement ring because I kept bumping the diamond against my desk or chair or matting it with soil when I was gardening. This simple piece of gold reminds me of Rob and how easy he made it for me to be with my parents this week.

On my right middle finger is a ring Mom and Dad gave to me when I graduated from law school. It's an inexpensive gold band with a tiny diamond chip placed next to a bright aqua opal. More beautiful in the eye of the beholder than it would be valuable to a dealer, the blue of the gem grows deeper and more complex every year.

I close my eyes tightly, allowing me to feel Dad without having to see his worried face. For the first time this week, I don't want the trip to end, and I especially don't want it to end for Dad.

By eleven o'clock, our plane has landed, we have collected our bags, climbed into Rhonda's car, and stepped through the door of the Iowa farmhouse once again. Back in friendly and familiar territory, Mom quickly reclaims her self-confidence and finds her bearings. Dad hobbles from room to room, inspecting the mail, scanning the newspapers, and stoking up the fire. Mom stands next to him in front of the wood stove, both of them feeling thoroughly warm for the first time in days.

I wait for their final pronouncement, the one made at the conclusion of every vacation, that no matter where they have traveled or what they have seen, the preferred place, the best place on the planet, is right here at home.

As if on cue, Dad makes his declaration, "It sure is good to be home."

I expected him to say this, but he catches me off guard with his next sentence.

"But I sure am glad we went."

My mind replays the past days I have just spent with my parents. It wasn't a bad vacation, just not quite the adventure any of us had envisioned when we first made plans last August. All the splendor of the landscape was witnessed through the front windshield of a Buick LeSabre. Dad struggled in and out of the car and never was able to steer the car where he wanted it to go. His pain exhausted his sense of adventure and made it impossible for him to explore almost anything but sleep. And we didn't see one single bear.

Despite these setbacks, Dad's focus tonight is on how fantastic it was he could make the trip at all. By his statement, he tells me that even as good as home feels to him now, he made the right choice, accepted the consequences of the risks, and couldn't feel better about his decision two and a half years ago to rip that brightly colored band from his wrist and live life as long and as full as possible.

Epilogue

April 12

By late January after we returned from our trip, Dad was feeling worse than usual. He visited the medical clinic for relief, but the doctor explained that the cancer was too aggressive for any other therapies. He had nothing else to offer Dad except medications to manage the pain.

Once they returned home, Dad inched out of the driver's side, and a sharp ping shot through his right leg. As the x-rays showed later, the cancer, or maybe the chemotherapy, had spun a honeycomb out of his bone, extending from his thigh down to his ankle. When Dad rotated his hip to step out of the car, the bone splintered like shards of glass and pulled apart.

"I can't do this anymore," he told Rhonda when she found Dad at the Council Bluffs hospital. "I just can't take this pain." If death could have released him from his agony, he would have welcomed it gladly.

I joined Dad and the rest of the family on the orthopedic floor late that same night. Two weeks previously, I had visited him on the cancer floor where he had been admitted for another blood transfusion. By this time, I had no trouble finding my way around the hospital.

The pain medications were taking effect, and Dad was much more lucid by the time I arrived than he was when Rhonda first saw him.

"They're going take it off, Rin," he said rationally and calmly, as if he were replacing a part on one of his tractors.

Dad's hip was already full of metal pins from when he broke it trying to protect the sweet corn from the raccoons. Nothing remained to which they could attach the lower bone. Also, this latest break scattered bone fragments through his lower leg, threatening to pierce an artery or vein.

The amputation was not optional, but the doctors made it clear that given Dad's fragile condition, Dad should prepare himself for all probable consequences.

No surgery would be done until Dad's blood thinner was out of his system or at least greatly reduced. Our family passed the hours changing positions in the hospital room chairs and sofa. Neighbors brought in baskets of food. Friends bearing flowers and cards stayed to visit and shared the latest gossip. The hours grew tedious with our superficial conversations and lack of substantive activity.

During one of those hours, while everyone else in the family was attending to personal errands, I found myself alone with Dad in the hospital room. I felt lucky to have this private time and sat in a brown metal chair between the side of his bed and the outside window.

He was awake, but the pain medication made it difficult for him to open his eyes. He kept them closed with his hands folded across his chest. He was in his typical sleeping position except for the steel rods and a pulley system immobilizing his right leg. Plastic tubes grew from the port previously inserted above his heart for easier chemotherapy sessions.

While he nodded off, hummed, or jiggled his left foot from side to side, I studied the square-tiled ceramic floor and listened to the sounds of the unknown machines in the hallway. Even though I had yarn and needles with me, I had no desire to knit. I only wanted to sit beside my father.

When he was alert, I felt compelled to ask him as many questions as would come to my mind. My inquiries seemed shallow, though, much like our Yellowstone conversations in the car. I asked about people and events, questions to which I already knew the answers.

After wasting enough time, I mustered up enough courage to ask something more substantive.

"Do you feel cheated by the cancer? That it's unfair to miss out on so much more of your life?"

With deliberate seriousness, he answered, "Well, Rin, you know the golden part about this whole thing is that everyone has to go through it."

He didn't necessarily mean everyone endures cancer, but that eventually we all face mortality.

The telephone on the table next to him interrupted us. Mom needed to know where some expense receipts were located. March first was a tax deadlines for farmers, and Mom needed to get the papers to the accountant.

"They're in that shoe box on the left side of my desk." Despite his sensory-numbing drugs, Dad still knew the exact locations of his financial papers.

Rhonda walked into the room as Dad hung up the phone. Wanting to leave my morbid questions behind, Dad joked, "You're just in time, Rhonda. We're just sitting here talking about the two certain things in life, death and taxes. Primarily the former, although I'm not sure which is going to arrive first."

The night before the surgery, a prayer service was held at the tiny white church where my parents attended each week. Relatives, neighbors, friends, and farmers all showed up to tell their favorite "Charles" story.

The sincere outpouring of love overwhelmed Dad. His spirits lifted when we repeated the generous praise and admiration of his friends, although he mockingly protested, "I'm not dead yet."

After a few more hours of stories and outright laughing, a nurse dressed in light blue scrub pants and a print smock broke the spell and presented Dad with the surgery consent form, reminding us that death was one of the probable consequences of the procedure. He signed, and she left us alone in the room, just my parents and their four children. Having only the six of us together was highly unusual and we treasured it. Before we left for the night, we encircled Dad's bed and joined our hands together. We were transported back to the farm living room, standing under the ceiling fan on the eve of one of us about to depart on a long journey. We each said prayers in our own way. Regardless of different religious philosophies, this powerful and peaceful moment provided us with a closeness we had been seeking since Dad first told us about the cancer.

The words of Dad's friends from the prayer service were more effective than any medicine Dad had ever received. The amputation surgery lasted only an hour, and the doctors were impressed with how well Dad tolerated the procedure and recovery.

In the two months immediately following the surgery, Dad felt the best he had felt in years. Apart from the phantom pains of which he had been warned, Dad was free of the constant throbbing in his right leg. He moved through the house more quickly now with his walker than he had before. Without chemotherapy, his appetite also improved.

More than ever he enjoyed visits and cards from friends. He spent long days following Mom around the house dressed in his white T-shirt and uncharacteristic sweat pants that fit comfortably around his severed limb. When a close neighbor died, Dad insisted on driving Mom and himself to the funeral.

Dad laughed louder than we had heard in years when Keasen couldn't figure out where to put Grandpa's other shoe. When we learned that Cyn was pregnant with her second child, we were thrilled by the news but grieved that Dad would never have the joy of meeting his youngest grandchild.

Time eventually ran out. I had time to prepare, but I still wasn't ready for him to die. I wasn't ready to face his absence every Thanksgiving when I saw his empty chair. I knew my children would soon remember their grandfather only in the context of a handful of stories, the same way I remember my grandfathers.

Surrounded by his family, Dad died in the very early hours of this morning. He died here at home, literally feet away from where he was born. In the predawn light, we search for appropriate conversation until the hospice nurse arrives and leads us through whatever is next.

I sit beside his empty body now, allowing emotions and memories to overwhelm me. I am suddenly desperate to memorize every detail of my time with Dad.

One conversation in particular plays over and over in my mind. It was from the day I was alone with Dad in the hospital asking him questions.

"Dad, do you remember how you felt when your parents died?"

"Oh my, yes," he answered quickly. Then he paused for a moment before speaking very thoughtfully and deliberately.

"I felt so alone when they died. I missed talkin' to them and doin' things with them. I missed them terribly. I still do."

Then, as if I was no longer in the room, he said to himself, "I miss them every single day."

I whisper to him now, certain that he can hear me.
"Me, too, Dad. I miss you, too."

www.ingramcontent.com/pod-product-compliance
Lightning Source LLC
Chambersburg PA
CBHW020514100426
42813CB00030B/3239/J